D1446279

André Breton

Twayne's World Authors Series

David O'Connell, Editor
Georgia State University

TWAS 117

ANDRÉ BRETON
by Henri Cartier-Bresson. Used by permission of Magnum Photos.

André Breton

Mary Ann Caws

Graduate School of the City University of New York

Twayne Publishers
An Imprint of Simon & Schuster Macmillan
New York
Prentice Hall International
London Mexico City New Delhi Singapore Sydney Toronto

Twayne's World Authors Series No. 117

André Breton
Mary Ann Caws

Twayne Publishers
An Imprint of Simon & Schuster Macmillan
1633 Broadway
New York, New York 10019

Library of Congress Cataloging-in-Publication Data
Caws, Mary Ann.
    André Breton / by Mary Ann Caws.   Updated ed.
        p.   cm. — (Twayne's world authors series ; no. 117)
    Includes bibliographical references and index.
    ISBN 0-8057-4623-4 (cloth : alk. paper)
    1. Breton, André, 1896–1966—Criticism and interpretation.
    I. Title. II. Series: Twayne's world authors series ; TWAS 117.
PQ2603.R35Z6513 1996
841'.912—dc20   95-44929
                                                                          CIP

10 9 8 7 6 5 4 3 2 1
Printed in the United States of America

Once, when I was alone, Jacqueline Lamba gave me André Breton's first loveletter to her; it was wrapped so that I did not know its contents, and she asked me to open it at midnight in Barcelona. For that gift, which I have kept as solemnly and joyously as she offered it, I dedicate this book to her, as I did my translation of Mad Love *so many years ago. She is dead and will not mind.*

Contents

Preface

I have more confidence in this present moment of my thought than in all the meaning people will try to give to a complete work, to a human life once it is finished.

—Manifestos

In rewriting my earlier book on André Breton, of 1971, I have had the occasion to rethink my point of view, to clarify some points which had remained murky in my mind, and to stress others, which I now find of crucial significance. To have such an occasion is particularly gratifying when it concerns a writer who wanted above all, to leave his life and works *open* to view. Like a glass house, he would say; like one of the great glass-enclosed *passages*, I think, as in *The Paris Peasant*, so that you can pass through, like a poem.

"This present moment of my thought": the reader is invited to speak, also, in the present moment, for such an author of openness. To put a limiting interpretation on his writing or being would be to set it within limits, to close it off to possibilities, that is, to the very thing to which he dedicated his life. The crucial metaphors with which his ideas, changing as they were, are joined—those swinging doors, communicating vessels, and connecting wires which haunt all the texts, theories, and attitudes of the Surrealist movement he led—militate against any too-simple explanation. Surrealism insists that every act is its own justification—is unique and *dissimilar.* We cannot assimilate it as a movement, for that would render it static. Poetry, said Breton, must be impenetrable.

Surrealism insists on the *latent content* and not on the manifest content, on the *interior necessity* and not on the exterior influences, on the *interior model* and not on the exterior representation. To look at this "mental situation" from the outside is already a dubious enterprise, and so I have taken, without any apology required, a halfway point as mine—in and out. To concentrate solely on the "influences" upon Surrealism, or upon its own reverberations in "influencing" fields beyond it, would betray Surrealism's essential and vitalizing spirit. Surrealism insists that every act is its own justification, is unique and *dissimilar.* We cannot assimilate it as a movement, for that would render it static.

In his "Lettre aux voyantes" ("Letter to the Mediums") of 1929, Breton urged the recognition of an *absolute possibility,* which was to furnish the basis of a moral truth. An epoch lived through may be more or less terrible, but to emphasize unduly the exterior variations detracts, like an undue emphasis on the past, from the crucial openness to the future. A device which claims to predict the so-called variability of the weather or of the times[1] is in error, for neither the past moments nor the present unrest or calm can determine the time to come. The future will or will not make itself felt as a guiding force in the present, depending on our hope:

> already the person I will be takes the person I am by the throat, but the person I have been leaves me in peace ("Letter to the Mediums,"[2] *OC* I, p. 908).[2]

The essential of humans living and imagining, Breton stated again and again, is their ability to "go beyond their human condition." For that reason alone, among so many others, Surrealism is not best served by a concentration on its past or present circumstances, on its history or its current difficulties.[3]

After a very brief discussion, therefore, of the *position* of Breton and Surrealism, of the variations of that position, and of the theoretical attitudes entailed, the order of this book will correspond chronologically to the texts left by Breton. In his *Nadja* he made a point of setting down facts and details "without a preestablished order"; so, within this rough chronology of chapters, I will refer in all freedom to other chapters. The two final sections—devoted to, respectively, three short essays of great importance and a few poetic texts—will form the basis of a few concluding remarks on Breton's attitude toward the image and the imagination, the alchemical operation on language and the world, and the future of poetry.

The translations used are, wherever possible, from the published translations of the works. Anything not yet published is my own translation.

Chronology

1896   Born in Tinchebray (Orne).

1915   After studies in medicine, Breton is mobilized. Serves in neuropsychiatric centers.[1]

1919   *Mont de Piété*. With Louis Aragon and Philippe Soupault, founds *Littérature,* where the "first" Surrealist text appears, *Les Champs magnétiques* (Breton and Soupault).

1919–1921   Participates in the Mouvement Dada.

1921   Marries Simone Kahn.

1922   Takes over direction of *Littérature*. Hypnotic sleep experiments. Editor of *La Révolution surréaliste* (see his explanation: "Why I am assuming the editorship of *La Révolution surréaliste*").

1924   *Manifeste du surréalisme*. Opening of the Bureau de Recherches Surréalistes, rue de Grenelle. *Au Grand Jour,* pamphlet signed by the Surrealists.

1928   Publication of *Nadja*.

1929   Editor of *Le Surréalisme au service de la révolution;* period of association with the Communist party.

1930   *Deuxième Manifeste du surréalisme;* denunciation of Antonin Artaud and Robert Desnos. *L'Immaculée Conception* (with Paul Eluard), simulation of the language of certain nervous disorders.

1932   *Les Vases communicants, Le Revolver à cheveux blancs.* Pamphlet, *Misère de la poésie* (on the Aragon affair). Founding of the new magazine *Minotaure*.

1934   May 29, "La Nuit du tournesol": meets Jacqueline Lamba, who will become his second wife, under circumstances he had predicted 11 years earlier in the poem "Tournesol" (see *L'Amour fou*). *L'Air de l'eau.*

1935   Goes to the Canary Islands, and to Prague. Rupture with the Communist party.

1936   Organizes International Surrealist Exhibition in London.

1937   *L'Amour fou.*

1938   Organizes International Exhibition of Surrealism in Paris. Goes to Mexico, where he founds, with Leon Trotsky, the Fédération Internationale de l'Art Indépendant Révolutionnaire; Trotsky asks that Diego Rivera's name be substituted for his own on the manifesto.

1940   *Anthologie de l'humour noir.* Goes to Marseilles, writes *Fata Morgana* there.

1941   Leaves for New York. Speaker for Voice of America; founds *VVV* with Marcel Duchamp, David Hare, Max Ernst.

1942   International Exhibition of Surrealism in New York.

1945   *Arcane 17* (set in the Gaspé Peninsula). Marries Elisa Bindhoff. Visits Southwest (background for the *Ode à Charles Fourier*) and Haiti, where his lecture touches off a general strike.

1946   Returns to Paris.

1947   International Exhibition of Surrealism in Paris, Galerie Maeght. Manifestation at the lecture of Tristan Tzara, "Le Surréalisme et l'après-guerre," which accuses the Surrealists and mainly Breton of nonrelevance to political events. Publication of *Ode à Charles Fourier.*

1948   Adheres to Front Humain (which later become Citoyens du Monde).

1949   Exposes fake Rimbaud, "La Chasse spirituelle," on grounds of interior evidence (see essay "Flagrant Délit").[2]

1950   Refuses Grand Prix de la Ville de Paris.

1952   Founding of *Médium.*

1953   *La Clé des champs.*

1955   *Prolégomènes à un troisième manifeste ou non.* "Du Surréalisme en ses oeuvres vives."

1956   Founding of *Le Surréalisme, même.*

1960   Execution of the Last Will and Testament of the Marquis de Sade.

1961   Founding of *La Brêche, action surréaliste.*

1966   Breton dies in Paris.

(NOTE: Breton's contributions to, and collaboration with, several journals besides those mentioned is of prime importance—from *Nord-Sud* on. See the longer works on him for details.)

Chapter One
Life, Youth, Revolution

Breton in the Present Tense

Breton tells us very little of his childhood; it is not a matter of importance for him, or for us. Those accustomed to standard biographies and autobiographies, with an unfailing number of early scenes, tedious descriptions of parents, painful portraits of the child in family groups and school groups, may see this as an odd gap. But to the reader who is in the slightest acquainted with the Surrealist disposition, such standard equipment would seem at best satirical, and more probably, ludicrous. Few Surrealists lament knowing little of the life of Lautréamont: the silence serves his reputation and nourishes his legend. Thus, the cover illustration of Patrick Waldberg's book on Surrealism, representing the author as a small boy, is a superb example of para-Surrealist humor. And Breton was often accused of having no sense of humor (he admitted, in the *First Manifesto*, being thought "as tedious as the rain").

In any event, what counts in any study of Breton is not his physical whereabouts—whether he is living in the Hôtel des Grands Hommes or 42 rue Fontaine, whether he is in Canada or in Arizona—or even his encounters and adventures as such. Only his state of mind is significant; it is generally accepted that even when it is the most clearly turned out toward or against the world, Surrealism is essentially a way of perceiving and reacting, and that its interest lies as much, if not more, in its own reactions and perceptions as in the situation that provokes them.

Of the period 1916–20, that is, the period immediately preceding the first surge of Surrealism, we are told more. During those four years, Breton emerges from the influences of Mallarmé and Valéry, perhaps through the contact in the neuropsychiatric ward at Nantes with Jacques Vaché, who accuses the "*pohète*"[1] in him and succeeds in turning him away from the path of "aestheticism" and "literature" toward a more revolutionary one. This turn can be traced in his intellectual path leading through the journals *Nord-Sud* and *Littérature* (whose title, as it is usually interpreted, is already satiric) toward the all-important titles of

La Révolution surréaliste and *Le surréalisme au service de la Révolution*. Breton's contact with Tristan Tzara and the Dada movement (1917–22) was certainly a decisive factor in his later development—whether or not it is considered *the* decisive factor depends on one's point of view. It is an indisputable fact that many of the themes and attitudes of Dada statements are found also in Surrealism, as will be apparent in this study. We may consider the encounter with Tzara and Dada itself to be, for the young men who were potential Surrealists, principally a state of readiness for the later development, as Breton would have us consider it; or we may take the view, as do some Dada sympathizers, that Breton builds up the legend of Vaché in order to reduce his apparent debt to Tzara and Dada. Luckily, there is no way of settling such disputes. Like the deliberate omission of details about the youth of Breton, uncertainty contributes to the aura of Surrealism itself.

In any case, Breton participates until 1921 in the various Dada demonstrations and manifestations, usually called "negative," and then tries to hold a Congress for the Determination of the Modern Spirit, usually thought of as an attempt to give a "positive" or constructive basis to an endeavor which until that time had been more or less formless. The more "orthodox" Dadaists oppose such an idea as essentially non-Dada, and the friction that has been latent among certain members of differing tendencies comes to the surface.

For the next few years, the future Surrealist group, led by Breton, concentrates above all on techniques of communication with the unconscious: the period of automatic writing, hypnotic slumber, counting of dreams, and the Bureau de Recherches surréalistes. After the influence of Freud came the influence of Marx; the subsequent period, roughly from 1929 to 1935, when the Surrealists align themselves with the French Communist party, can be considered a more "practical" period—except for Eluard and Aragon, it was of short duration, due in part to the personality of Breton, and then to his temperamental as well as political alignment with Trotsky, whom he visited, with Jacqueline Lamba, in Mexico. (A vestmental detail: it is from this period, when they spent time with the artists Diego Rivera and Frida Kahlo, that Jacqueline started wearing the kind of long skirts Frida wore—during the time I knew her, and we visited back and forth, she was always clothed like this.)

During the war years, Breton, whose anthology of black humor is banned in Vichy France, goes first to Marseilles, then to New York to broadcast for the Voice of America. In New York the Surrealist group with new members continues its meetings with enthusiasm, and Breton founds the journal *VVV* with David Hare. He travels widely (to the Southwest, to the Canary Islands, to Canada) and writes works of a more mystic inclination, in the vein of his *Fata Morgana*, written before his departure from Marseilles. His *Ode to Charles Fourier* extols the "sense of festival," with all its gnostic and joyously communal implications. His magnificently lyric *Arcane 17*, written in the Gaspé Peninsula, is itself an ode to love—for his new companion Elisa, who was to become his wife—and to the mysteries of the alchemical and the arcane.

On his return to France, Breton once more forms a Surrealist group but is now under attack by Tzara and others for having chosen exile over resistance. Although the friction with the Communist party continues, Breton and the Surrealists sign, with some Communist members, political declarations such as the statement of the hundred and one intellectuals for Algerian independence. During Breton's life, and after his death, the Surrealists never cease to speak out for various liberal causes; the tone of their periodicals, *Médium, Le Surréalisme, même, La Brêche*, and *Archibras*, is not unlike that of *La Révolution surréaliste*.

At the end of his life, Breton, enfeebled, suffering badly from asthma, entrusts the leadership of the group to some of the young Surrealists. Two months before his death, a ten-day meeting of the Surrealist group and several commentators on Surrealism is held in Normandy (at Cerisy-la-Salle). Although Breton takes a great interest in the meeting, he is unable to attend, but the vociferous and enthusiastic disputes there prove that Surrealism has lost none of its energy; Jean Schuster, one of the leading younger Surrealists, is in touch with Breton by telephone every evening, as I remember it. During the 1968 May–June events in France, the Surrealists take a position far more revolutionary than that of the French Communist party (see the special number of *Archibras* for the occasion). Breton would not have disapproved.

Breton and Others

On one point, the completely opposed views of Breton's critics are especially interesting: his attitude toward youth. Breton was until the moment of his death eager to show his appreciation of the new, of the young, of the revolutionary. Claude Mauriac, son of the famous Catholic novelist François Mauriac, accuses him of having favored the most imitative and most pathetic manifestations out of a real fear of underestimating any human possibilities. Breton the critic, says Mauriac along with a number of others, went beyond what he knew and even beyond what he genuinely thought. "Having been in the avant-garde, and having been unanimously recognized for its leader, he never stopped being afraid that he might be left behind. Whence his inconceivable indulgence in the face of the most frivolous attempts of an untalented youth, to whom he always tends to give credit, just because it is youth and because it claims to be revolutionary."[2]

And on the other side, Victor Crastre contends that Breton's generosity to movements that and persons who might have gone beyond Surrealism in some way should be seen as of primary importance. Referring to one of the passages where Breton claims that he would be the first to desert Surrealism if he found it to lag behind some other current of thought, Crastre remarks, "I am not a Surrealist, Breton would say at the very moment when his attitude would be the most Surrealist attitude imaginable."[3]

No judgments of this sort will be made in the following pages. That Breton was generous toward others when perhaps he ought not to have been, that he was at other times perhaps wrongly ungenerous—different readers will find these things touching, understandable, or unforgivable, depending mainly on their attitude toward Breton as a person, and toward Surrealism as the movement which he formed, and with which he is so closely identified.

Chapter Two
André Breton and Surrealism

Later on you will learn who we are.
—"Ligne brisée" ("Broken Line"), *The White-Haired Revolver*

The Moment and the Group

Breton says of his own "very sinuous path" that it

passes through Heraclitus, Abelard, Eckhardt, Retz, Rousseau, Swift, Sade, Lewis, Arnim, Lautréamont, Engels, Jarry, and some others. I have made for myself a system of coordinates, a system which has withstood my personal experiences and therefore seems to me to include some chances for tomorrow. ("Prolegomena to a Third Manifesto," *Manifestes du surréalisme*, 342)[1]

To this catalog of authors invoking, variously, mysticism, alchemy, antibourgeois revolution, black humor, eroticism, and reliance on the play of contraries—all elements which are easily discerned in Surrealist works in general and in Breton's work in particular—it is easy to add a few others. Freud (with the restrictions discussed later) and the importance of the unconscious; Hegel and the dialectical process as well as the idea of the hegemony of poetry over the arts; Rimbaud and the disorientation of the senses as well as the "anguishing" split between the self speaking and the other self, and the importance of language as evocation and incantation. Of course, at certain moments, the occult takes precedence over the theoretical ideal, just as in the early days of Surrealism the emphasis falls on automatic processes for transcribing the relevations of the unconscious, while later Breton begins a discussion of "The Automatic Message" with a declaration about the history of automatism as a regrettable series of misfortunes. However, he continues to put his faith in the spontaneous as revelatory. The French word "histoire" can be misleading, for it can be read also as "story"—so that interpretation is at least, and as often, double. The story permits, in any case, a certain continuous faith, in spite of the vicissitudes involved. "I proclaim in this

5

matter the right to absolute severity. No concessions to the world and no forgiveness. *"With the terrible bargain in our hands"* (*Manifestes,* 21). If the fault is with the "history" of past Surrealist attitudes, then it only proves the necessity of relying on the present moment rather than on past commitment: "Each full moment carries within itself the negation of centuries of limping and broken history" ("Prolegomena to a Third Manifesto or Not," in *Manifestes,* 343). We know from the *First Manifesto* that Breton takes *no account of the nul moments* in his life, he simply rules them out, for himself and for us: "I want anyone who feels nothing," he says, "to shut up. It was Dostoeyevski's mistake to include descriptions of everyday moments; let us not fall into that one" (*OC* I, 314–15).

In addition to the names already cited, that of Marx should be mentioned as another to whom Breton owed obvious allegiance; the reasons for this allegiance are clear. The act of reinterpreting the work must be linked to the activity of transmuting the world, to use the alchemical term to which Breton was so attached. Or, as he puts it, "'Transform the world,' said Marx; 'change life,' said Rimbaud: these two goals make only one for us" ("Discourse to the Congress of Writers," 1935, *OC* II, 459).

All the Surrealists quote Lautréamont's statement that poetry must be made by all (and, adds Breton, it must be heard by all, although this point is one on which the attitude differs, as has already been obvious— it depends on the *moment*).[2] Their work is at all times a work in common, their attitude is the attitude of a group, implying as that does certain peculiar strengths and other peculiar weaknesses. For instance, on the positive side, their cooperation leads to work that could not have come from one brain alone, metaphors whose *valeur secouante,* or disturbance quotient, depends on their multiple origins.

Politics

Two things must still be said, or rather, touched on, about Surrealism as a whole. First, the history of its relations with the Marxist revolution of class struggle; for a time in the early 1930s, the Surrealists allied themselves with the Communists in the hope of achieving a definite conciliation between the two movements ("revolutions"), but various irritations occurred. Breton publicly defended an anarchistic poem of Aragon's ("Le Front rouge") as poetry, first as "occasional verse," therefore not to be taken seriously on a political level, and later as poetry, so set apart from public judgment (see the pamphlet *Misère de la poésie*). Under pressure (according to some historians), Aragon, having just returned from the Soviet Union, renounced Breton's defense of him and his poem—which he had intended part of the *real* world—and split off from the Surrealists. The repercussions were great; protests on one side or the other came in from all over the world, insisting that the "content" of a poem be restricted to the realm of poetry, or refusing to relegate it only to that realm. That Breton himself should have been assigned to a cell of gas workers and given the dullest sort of work to do seems to indicate that the French Communist party was never to have great faith in the Surrealists, whose party allegiance was, so it appeared to them, more a poetic attitude than a practical commitment.

After 1935, the Surrealists broke with the Communists, while retaining their strong Marxist inclinations and fervent admiration for Trotsky, with whom Breton wrote, in Mexico, a manifesto concerning the freedom of art. It was signed by Diego Rivera for political reasons and from prudence. Although the Surrealists and the Communists have at times taken the same positions, there remains a good deal of animosity between them. At the time of the May 1968 student and worker uprising in France, the Surrealists wrote vituperative manifestos against the "nonrevolutionary" attitude of the Communist party.

If one follows Breton's own remarks on the subject, his attitude is perfectly clear and consistent. For him, we should all be in permanent revolt against limits of all kinds. To accept as a goal of revolution a specific condition (such as the overthrowing of a class or the furnishing of satisfactory material benefits to all) is to limit that revolution, to set a possible term on it. At various times he and the other Surrealists also protest against the *use* of art for "propaganda" (not only on one side, but on any side, including the "good" side; see Benjamin Péret's *Dishonor of Poetry*, an attack on a volume of Resistance poetry called *L'Honneur des poètes*, as confusing uplifting sentiment with poetic expression). Art cannot be used, it must be free; here Breton quotes the young Marx on the necessary liberty of the pen. Freedom of the mind, from the Surrealist point of view, is even more important than freedom from hunger. Nevertheless, in the alternations which characterize Surrealism—and wanting to avoid the art-for-art's sake aesthetic—Breton insists that any painting must hold its own in a world of famine, must bear juxtaposition with the greatest human suffering if it is to be worth anything at all.

"Existence is elsewhere." Nothing matters if it is not the "annihilation of being in a *blind and interior diamond.*" This distance once placed between Surrealists and their world, between exterior appearance and interior brilliance, may seem to vary, but to some extent its effect is always present. In later life, Breton had a pronounced mystical streak, often putting him at odds with the practical. The alchemical process, to which he often compared the poetic process, is literally devoted to the producing of the interior diamond. The alternations between the attitudes of poetry-for-all and of prevent-the-public-from-entering have already been mentioned: the difficulty lies very deep, far too deep for anyone not connected with the movement to do more than mention it.

Breton, the acknowledged leader of the group until his death, and the man whose spirit is alive among group members still, provides the most interesting focus for a study of Surrealism. His major ideas are present in his *Entretiens,* a series of conversations over the years 1913–52,[3] his public talks, such as the "Political Position of Art Today," "Discourse to the Congress of Writers," and the numerous texts on which the present volume is based.

Ethics and Aesthetics

The Dada movement, with which Breton was allied before the formation of the Surrealist group, is considered to have *only* made fun of art as a simply aesthetic process and product. Yet, the Dada essays on poetry and on visual art written by Tristan Tzara, the guiding spirit of the movement, are in reality just as positive as they are negative.[4] They are always brightly colored, funny, and full of mordant wit.

"Art is liquidating itself as are countries," says Breton in an early Dada essay ("Distances," in *Lost Steps*). All the Surrealists, including Breton, were certainly anti aesthetics as aesthetics. But in Surrealism, poetry is never to be attacked, only the "art" of prose. All Surrealist work, from the point of view of its content, is poetic, since the Surrealist attitude is identified by the Surrealists themselves with the poetic or "lyric" attitude. Poetry is an attitude, not a form. Prose depreciates the world, and language; poetry, really an ethical attitude rather than an aesthetic one, exhilarates both.

Some of the great figures in Surrealism are judged in these lights. Paul Eluard, for example, while he was the colleague Breton preferred— and even before he became a hardish-line Marxist—was finally to be distrusted, as privileging the poem too much as an aesthetic object in itself (*C,* 82). It is true, for Breton, that the poetic statement must remain impenetrable (*C,* 127), but that was not to declare it merely aesthetic.

The severity of discipline and the clash of personalities were and still are responsible for difficulties that do not always involve only the theory of Surrealism. From the beginning, Surrealism as conceived by Breton was a totally uncompromising movement. The positions taken and the theories stated all had a remarkable quality of certainty and of a highly moral commitment. When members were excluded, the reason given usually was that they had in some way compromised, either with journalism (as in the case of Robert Desnos), or with public favor (in the case of Max Ernst, whose acceptance of a prize was considered by the Surrealists a complete indignity and a betrayal of Surrealist purity). Members are exiled (Artaud, Desnos), hard feelings are generated (Aragon, Breton), ex-members are forgiven (see Breton's remarks on Tzara and on Desnos), and then different members, or the same ones, leave the group for political reasons (Tzara, Eluard). The reasons become increasingly complicated in hindsight. For example, Antonin Artaud, the great silent film actor, prose poet, and theoretician of *The Theatre and Its Double,* whom Breton says he will always remember "with policemen on either side," was distrusted by Breton not only for his bourgeois attitude, but still more for his fever pitch of imagination and the *abstraction* it demanded and offered. This last is, I think, an interesting distrust, emphasizing Breton's own sensual delight in the here and now, the pleasurable earthly stuff of living:

> The space that Artaud led me into always strikes me as abstract, a hall of mirrors. For me, there's always something "verbal" about it, even if that verb is very noble, very beautiful. It's a place of lacunae and ellipses in which, personally, I lose all my means of communication with the innumerable things that, despite everything give me pleasure and bind me to this earth. (*C,* 86)

As for Aragon, whose eventual total commitment to Communism put him outside the Surrealist group, he proved—for Breton—too much of a literalist, as seen in his interpretation of one of Dali's Surrealist objects. (Now Dali himself, of course, was heartily despised by Breton and the others, who called him AVIDA DOLLARS for his capitulation to the fashion world by designing department store windows and the like. Worse than that, even, was what Breton called his "self-kleptomania" [*C,* 30], always repeating what he had already done.)[5] In this case, Dali had prepared a dinner jacket studded all over with whiskey glasses full of milk. "To the amazement of everyone present, Aragon vehemently protested the waste of this milk, and even went so far as to say that children might go hungry." While to us this may seem eminently sensible, this betrayed his non-Surrealist state of mind, according to those around

(*C*, 161). This did not mean that Breton was oblivious to poverty. He remembers, in his *Conversations,* writing "Ode à Charles Fourier," in Nevada, and especially in Arizona and New Mexico, where he was greatly impressed, among the Native Americans he met, by the "inalienable dignity and genius, which contrasted so sharply with their miserable living conditions." In any case, the diverse fallings-out of these and those with Breton can be followed in detail in the various and numerous histories of Surrealism.

What is more relevant to this study is the fact that Breton remained faithful to an image of himself as revolutionary and of Surrealism as a total and permanent revolt against accepted judgments and habits. Through the most obvious inconsistencies, this fidelity lends an undeniable unity to all his work. This unity of vision in no way entails a consistent viewpoint. Breton does not go so far as to stick behind all the statements he makes of an excessive type, such as the celebrated demand that the most Surrealist act is to "fire blindly into the crowd" upon the first people you see. He attributes this to a period of giddiness (*C*, 222), without trying to rationalize it away. Such excessive statements were clearly part of the romantic philosophy Surrealism was.[6]

In the group ethic Surrealism clung to, language was necessarily an impersonal construct. As one critic has pointed out, the very notion of automatic writing and drawing, those nonindividualistic exercises—like the game of the "exquisite corpse"—fits in with the ideal detachment from Western individualism characteristic of the Eastern thought to which they were attracted.[7] In the *cadavre exquis,* the players each draw a head, a neck, a torso, legs, and feet, one after the other, folding down the paper as they go, so that each addition is meant to surprise. If it is a verbal game, the players write a noun and adjective, a verb, another noun and adjective, depending on the number of players; the title comes from the first game played: "The exquisite corpse will drink the new wine." In every case, the whole, collective surprise is a kind of Surrealist revelation, like a *found object,* only this time not in the world outside, but in the world of the collective imagination.

This kind of group art responds to the ethical sense of the movement as a whole, moving past the individual to something larger: a concern with collective art and action.

Chapter Three
1924: *Lost Steps*

Freedom and Risk

The primary impulse for these essays, which cover the period of Dada through the separation of Tzara and the Surrealists, is once more the problem of freedom. "The Disdainful Confession" at the beginning of the collection is a haughty attack on the idea of human experience and *equilibrium,* that is, on man's instinctive assimilation or adaptation of things to himself and himself to things. Luckily, says Breton, the sense of equilibrium (or placidity) is disturbed when conditions no longer favor it, and this change of conditions is inevitable. The goal of the revolutionary artist or writer is to destroy, at least mentally, these conditions so as to liberate the human mind from this imprisoning self-satisfaction. Breton, twenty-seven years old, claims that he has not known such equilibrium for a long time, and that the same could be said of all those who share in his mental aristocracy, which is equivalent to a state of unrest or disquiet. He, like his friends, refuses to adapt, to present a social face to social situations, to take comfort in any *belief,* because such "vulgar" compromise would betray the spirit of Surrealism. The creed of these unadaptables is stated, categorically, on the first page of the essay:

> Absolutely incapable of settling for the fate allotted to me; struck in my highest degree of awareness by the denial of justice that the notion of original sin, to my mind, in no way excuses; I refuse to adapt my existence to the pitiful conditions under which everyone *here below* must exist. (*OC* I, 193)

The terms are, as always, extreme: *"absolument," "aucunement," "dérisoire," "ici-bas."* The Dada revolution was supposed to be a highly moral revolution, as Tzara and the other Dadaists agree. It might have seemed a purely frivolous manifestation against the bourgeois culture and civilization to whose bankruptcy World War I bore witness, but it was profoundly moral in its deliberately scandalous attacks on all it found scandalous. It is in moral concerns that Breton feels he always

11

found his "main subjects of exaltation."[1] The passage from the absolute to the relative and from doubt to negation must somehow be made without sacrificing moral values. Consistency of thought or expression matters little, because inconsistency is an honest indication of the contradictions Breton finds everywhere in the human character and the human condition; these contradictions reflect the inescapable dualities that he calls the "marvelous wound" revealed by Rimbaud ("Characteristics of the Modern Evolution and What It Consists Of," *OC* I, 294[2]). What matters above all is the basic morality of the concern.

In this respect, the Dada/Surrealist conception of poetry surpasses even philosophy as it goes past practical utility, and any traditional concept of poetry, in its effort to restore content to form. Breton insists, for instance, that Racine's moral dissertations are absolutely "unworthy of the admirable expression they adopt." For him, poetry is, in spite of all its disappointments, the place where the terrible conflicts of consciousness and confidence in the individual mind have the best chance of being solved. In poetic language the equivocal can be maintained, whereas the nature of prose makes it less hospitable to the expression of dualities, resolved or not. The notion of the *equivocal* is a positive counterpart of the abhorred idea of *equilibrium.* If the balance is generative of a greater number of ideas, it is to be valued; but insofar as the balance of ideas lends stability, it must be rejected in the interest of Surrealist "vertigo." In a discussion of Lautréamont's *Chants de Maldoror,*[3] Breton describes the exhilaration of holding two opposing ideas *"en ballottage,"* in a perfect state of indecision, where both can be tossed about without a betrayal of one side for the other, without reduction or simplification. The active play of alternates is akin to the basic notion of dialectic, which appeals to Dadaists and Surrealists alike (*OC* I, 234).[4] The alternation of opposites is often reflected in their preference for a style of paradox, a style to which poetry and "poetic" prose are particularly well suited. When Breton defends his affection for poetry, in an extremely important passage of the essay "Clearly," he explains that, in his interpretation, the word has more to do with the lives of writers (or nonwriters) than with what they write or could write. And the definition he gives shows as well as any other group of terms his paradoxical style, speaking of the way in which an individual "seems to have accepted the unacceptable human condition" (135).

This is their definition of poetry as well as of human life at its best: both are based on an extreme consciousness of the equivocal and of the necessity (and even the beauty) of the absurdities of the "real." In his

"Disdainful Confession," Breton states his gratitude to Jacques Vaché[5] for having prevented him from being a *poet* in the traditional sense of the word. Poetry, for the Dadaists and the Surrealists, is a totally uncompromising attitude and never a pleasing series of words, or, even worse, rhymes. Poetry is, to take a lofty and yet typical example, Breton's refusal to be attached: "It used to be that I never left home without saying farewell to all the binding memories that had accumulated there, to everything that I felt ready to perpetuate in myself" (12). Poetry is the love of the unfinished, of things unaccomplished. Taking the opposite point of view from Montaigne, who said that man embraces too much and so ends up with nothing,[6] Breton answers that his goal is more than anything else to embrace everything. Poetry is the willingness to risk, *foolishly,* all the comfortable situations for a simple shadow and then to call the risk justified: "and it is enough, for the moment, that such a pretty shadow should be dancing on the ledge of the window out of which, each day, I'll begin by hurling myself once more" (*OC* I, 24). His repeated references to the future and to the repeated future of the act emphasize the promise and the frequency of the risk, while the sufficiency of the reward stated at the beginning contrasts with the shadowy reward itself and the extremity of the risk at the very end.

Breton's criticism of the Dada movement is based exactly on the minimum consequences of the risk. He complains in "Leave Everything" that Dada was for some a way out, a way not of adventuring but of remaining just where they were:

> Dadaism, like so many other things, was for certain people no more than a means of sitting down. . . . Ideas are neither good nor evil, they simply are. All the same to me whether they please or displease; they are much more worthy when they impassion me in one direction or another. Pardon me for thinking that, unlike ivy, I die when I become attached. (*OC* I, 263)

That the Dada movement should have ended not by a revolution, but in the windows of bookstores and in café discussions, is a terrible disappointment. He laments the extraordinary disproportion between the revolution in ideas and its negligible consequences in the world. Dada was a stranger to dialectic, and thus unaware of the essential connection between the inner activity of ideas and their outer results. The final admonition of Breton to his followers in the mental aristocracy of adventure is justly famous:

Leave everything.

Leave Dada.

Leave your wife, leave your mistress.

Leave your hopes and fears.

Drop your kids in the middle of nowhere.

Leave the substance for the shadow.

Leave behind, if need be, your comfortable life and promising future.

Take to the highways.

(*OC* I, 263)

Dada was useful to the Surrealists mainly as a way of keeping them unattached to anything, in a state of perfect *availability,* as Breton explains in "Clearly"; a retrospective statement, this is in no way contradicted by the attitude of the future Surrealists at the moment of their greatest enthusiasm for Dada. The opening paragraph of Breton's own essay "For Dada" is a protest against all limits imposed by mental habits and happenings exterior to him:

It is impossible for me to conceive of a mental joy other than as a breath of fresh air. How could it be comfortable within the limits in which nearly every book, every event confines it? I doubt that there is one single person who has not, at least once in his life, been tempted to deny the external world. He would then realize that nothing is so serious or definite as all that. He would move on toward a revision of moral values, which would not prevent him from then returning to common law. Those who paid for this marvelous moment of lucidity with permanent disorientation are still called poets: Lautréamont, Rimbaud—but the fact is, literary childishness ended with them. (*OC* I, 236)

Dada signified freedom not only from usual customs and bourgeois judgments, but also from all the imprisonments of logic and literature seen as *work.* "For Dada" reads as a celebration of the spontaneously created images that Breton calls *"trouvailles,"* or found things, connecting them to "inspiration," an old-fashioned term that he would like to put back into use. The notions of the innocent and the arbitrary stressed in this essay are also linked to the notion of freedom, for innocence implies the absence or denial of any previous knowledge or experience that might weigh down the mind. He puts an equal emphasis on the arbitrary, because chance implies the absence or denial of logical progression and order. Those who are sufficiently innocent to accept the arbitrary as a guide for living and writing have come to the realization that "nothing is so serious or definite as all that." After such a realization, it is possible, as Breton admits, for some to place themselves again under the "common law," that is, to continue to compromise with the experiences and logic of the outside world. But some do not, and they risk everything. Poetry as writing or living is no longer to be played with—a new terrorism, as Breton puts it, makes that impossible.

Doubt

Breton's "Two Dada Manifestos" contain terse and convincing descriptions of Dada "as a state of mind" in which all the former kinds of language are suddenly felt to be unworkable. This is only partly the deliberate choice of ambiguity and contradiction ("One has only to utter a sentence in order for the opposite sentence to become DADA"); it is more significantly a genuine realization of the psychological discrepancy between the speaker's wishes and his words ("I've seen Tristan Tzara lose his voice while asking for a pack of cigarettes at the tobacconist's"; "One can know the word Hello and still say Farewell to the woman one meets again after a year's separation") (*OC* I, 231). Language is the worst convention of all, and it is chiefly in our attack upon it that we are poets.

The terrain Dada chooses for its manifestations is the terrain of *doubt;* unfortunately, it is not always possible to define the precise boundaries chosen, or to prevent the doubt from turning against the person who uses it. The easier counterpart of doubt is the provocation of others. For Dada, provocation is always more valuable than acceptance, the shock of any statement contributing in large measure to its vitality. "A truth will always benefit from adopting an outrageous means of expression," says Breton in his 1922 speech in Barcelona (*OC* I, 291). Unfortunately, the provocation wears off rapidly. In our present cultural climate one cannot conceive any longer of a *"poésie maudite,"* because the most outlandish sentiments are immediately accepted as one more cultural phenomenon; once the absorption process of the larger culture starts, the originality of the protest vanishes in a common approval. Even though the writer of revolutionary tracts leaves no margins at the side of the pages or the mind—and Breton makes a point of saying that he himself leaves none—still the text will be watered down by the well-meaning public, always parasitic on the ideas of a few. Many of the metaphors used by the Dadaists and Surrealists are metaphors of violence, such as Breton's famous remark that the simplest Surrealist act would be to go down in the street and fire on the first passerby, a remark that he later claims to have made in a giddy frame of mind.

The Surrealists' attacks on the traditional places of culture are extreme: they call the museum where certain art objects are *consecrated* a place of entombment[7] and recommend instead the unplanned living performance of the streets or the planned and insulting performance of desecration. Of course, the same recommendation extends to educational institutions; for example, the Surrealist Robert Desnos calls for all amphitheaters (representing the imparting of traditional knowledge under traditional forms) to be deserted for the new adventure of the streets. Yet this is not sufficient as a permanent revolt. Historians of art will always hold exhibitions of Dada and Surrealist art within the museums themselves, and amphitheaters will always be used for lectures on Dada and Surrealism. Breton foresees this ultimate danger very clearly; in the essay "Distances" he laments that even the notion of *"inquiétude"* (unrest, mental discomfort) has become a system.

Although endeavoring not to "slip on the parquet floor of sentimentality" (*"After Dada"*) and not to permit Surrealism to make of itself a systematic structure (an accusation often leveled, which Breton always denied), Breton does nevertheless express a continuing faith in the *idea* as a generative force. He takes a position contrary to that of Picabia ("One must be a nomad," said Picabia, "crossing ideas as one crosses countries or towns") and maintains that, even if the risk is a silly one, "even if every idea were fated to disappoint us, I would still take it as my starting point to devote my life to them" (*OC* I, 261). Dada is usually said to have committed suicide in 1922 as a final negative or "pure" act (which justifies Breton's title *After Dada*), although Tzara refuses up until the end of his life to separate his early writings from his later ones by calling some "pre-Dada" and some "post-Dada." Dada was to him a continuing process, just as Surrealism considers itself a continuing quest: "'The place and the formula' might always elude me, but—and this can't be said often enough—the important thing is this search and nothing else" (*OC* I, 261).

Art and Language

Art is, for the Surrealists, a way of knowledge. Painting is useless insofar as it represents, useless when it tells us what we already know, and never valuable on purely aesthetic grounds:

> I persist in thinking that a painting or piece of sculpture can be conceived only secondarily from the viewpoint of taste, and holds its own only insofar as it is liable to take our abstract knowledge, properly speaking, a step forward. (*OC* I, 288)

In the essay "Distances," Breton bitterly denounces speculation in the art market as the most definite and least defensible absorption of revolution. But much of the blame falls on individual artists in their frequent misconception of the role of art; their ambition should lie in another realm altogether from that of Renoir, who could call the painting of a nude finished the moment he wanted to give its bottom a spank. Surely there are more interesting revelations to be gained from art than that, says Breton, and he concludes ironically:

> Just let me say that if we were to be influenced by that rather than by something else, we would not be where we are today: perhaps we would eat fewer apples and would not be forced to endure the proximity of that woman whom we have not invited, and whom we are tired of seeing lounging in more or less suggestive poses on our sofa. (*OC* I, 290)

All the Surrealist creates, then, should be the exact opposite of the representational painting of such artists as Cézanne and Renoir. Indeed, the two most important essays in this volume on what was to be called Surrealist writing (in homage to Apollinaire, although not to his "reactionary" play *Les Mamelles de Tirésias*)[8] make plain the enormous difference between the two conceptions of art. Nor should Surrealists permit themselves to be seduced into writing a novel with a thesis, a play with a thesis, and so on. Marcel Duchamp is to be admired for scorning every evident thesis or statement, as well as for his effective destruction of what Breton calls the "lyricism-blackmail of a ready-made expression." When Duchamp signs a manufactured object as if it were his own work, or when he bases all his decisions on a flip of the coin, his elevation of chance to the role art has been accustomed to playing, it is the most powerful revenge that could be taken on the accepted notion of aesthetics. It is interesting, though not often mentioned, that Breton issues a definite warning at this juncture about not falling into a new mystique of art. That the first wave of enthusiasm about automatic writing eventually subsides for the Surrealists does not imply a betrayal of what Surrealism once "stood for"; it is instead a testimony of Breton's fidelity to his own guiding principle.

But there is no doubt about the original enthusiasm. "Entry of the Mediums" describes the sense that Breton and his friends give to Surrealism as a psychic automatism that corresponds to the "state of dreaming," a state that he first illustrates in terms of his personal experience. Just before going to sleep, phrases or sentences with no obvious meaning would present themselves to his mind, and he judged these to be "poetic elements of the first order." He and Philippe Soupault were able to reproduce in themselves at will the state of abstraction from the outside world necessary to receive these "magic dictations" that came at such speed they had to take notes in shorthand in order not to lose any of the words.

The Magnetic Fields was the result of and commentary on their efforts, each chapter containing the recital of one day's dictation. In these pages Breton explains the risk haunting this exercise of the unconscious. One is endlessly and "maliciously" tempted to heed another voice besides that of the genuine unconscious, to change in some fashion, for such *exterior* reasons as the aesthetic or the logical, the dictates of the first voice, which should be "sufficient unto itself." Any change is a compromise, and all compromise is fatal to the spirit of Surrealism. In spite of feeling that this dictation could not be *used* for any specific purpose, Breton is persuaded at this point and for a long time to come "that nothing that is said or done is worth anything" unless it is said or done under the orders of the unconscious. The more conscious elements enter into a creation and are thereby placed under the law of a human will-to-literature, the less fruitful will be any discoveries and revelations forthcoming from the creation.

The second illustration Breton gives in this essay is that of his friends' attempts to capture the language of the unconscious in the "telling of dreams," that recounting of such supreme fascination. But there was always a built-in limit of usefulness, for the documents produced were neither numerous nor characteristic.

The third kind of experience, however, is found to be so remarkable that, to use Breton's dramatic but not insincere terms, "the most blasé among us, the most sure of themselves, are taken aback, tremble with gratitude and fear; it might be said that they have lost countenance before the marvel." Under the instruction of a medium, René Crevel had learned to put himself to sleep and in this state was able to speak in a more or less flowing discourse, a procedure subsequently attempted by the other Surrealists. But even before describing these hypnotic sleep experiments, Breton is careful to say that the Surrealists have never taken the "spiritualistic" attitude and that he refuses any possibility of communication between the living and the dead. One might wonder why he should bother to stress this particular point, since few people are in danger of confusing spiritualism with Surrealism, but, in any case, the distinction he draws continues to hold, even when the Surrealists insist on the priority of sensations over ideas. (Breton claims that the reason he writes poetry is to re-create within himself the emotions or *sensations* he feels upon reading or experiencing certain things, stating that *sensations* have always been of primary importance to him, although they have never been of the "mystical" type.)[9]

Breton recounts in some detail the first experiences with sleep-writing. Robert Desnos, having expressed the greatest doubt about his own capacity for such experiments, and having recently exposed two public hypnotists himself, suddenly drops his head on his arm and scratches the table convulsively, and then wakes up convinced that nothing unusual has transpired. The next day, when the experience is repeated, he writes, answers questions, and draws pictures, even though he ordinarily is unable to draw. Not all those in the group are successful at this: Breton makes a perfectly straightforward remark by Breton that he, Paul Eluard, Max Ernst, and Max Morise were never able to fall asleep under these conditions, although they would have wished to do so. That Breton should be so genuinely enthusiastic about an experiment in which he could not himself participate is, I think, testimony to his essential and initial, intuitive generosity of spirit. Some may find it more indicative of his credulity, just as one may suspect that Desnos and the others were occasionally prone to exaggerate and overdramatize in order to win Breton's full approval.[10] And some would suggest that it was Breton's eventual jealousy of Desnos about this and other matters that won out when he expelled Desnos from the movement.

The often quoted essay "Les Mots sans rides" is a convincing meditation on the newly discovered power of language and on the responsibility of the poet toward it. Words must no longer be considered simple and trustworthy auxiliaries to human thought—it is time for their liberation. To succeed in the verbal alchemy Rimbaud spoke of, Breton calls for a verbal chemistry to bring into existence all the possible meanings by scientific procedures. The word must be regarded as independent in itself and in its new relations with other words, and we must all refrain from attributing to it the properties we were accustomed to assigning it. The wrinkles shed by the words, which are now rejuvenated as they are freed from their long past, resemble the "pleats" in Breton's image of the young people who refuse *"le pli";* they are both symptoms of fixity, the enemy of all new movements. Out of their past grooves, words are suddenly weapons of the present and the future. Now language recovers its original purpose, that of "advancing knowledge, of exalting life" (167).

Equivalent to art in its contribution to the most genuine form of learning, poetic language intensifies and broadens the scope of life. Natural human conservatism in its horror of infinite freedom would impose a limitation and a dulling on linguistic experience, as on all other kinds; to this end it insists that well-groomed speech take into account before anything else the etymology of the word ("its deadest weight," says Breton), so that all the vibrations of meaning can be confined to a narrow range of order. The opposite of this attitude is called poetry.

When for the first time a specific color was assigned to each vowel sound (as in Rimbaud's "Sonnet à couleurs"), the word was diverted from its "duty" to signify, so that it could be born into a concrete, "architectural" existence.[11] The idea of freshness makes a paradoxical contrast with the idea of verbal "innocence," on which Breton claims we can no longer count. He means, of course, that we as users of language cannot now rely on the submission of language to us and to our preconceived ideas: "The important thing is that the alarm has been sounded, and that from now on it seems imprudent to speculate about the innocence of words" (OC I, 285). All the melodramatic images here ("alarm" implies danger, as does the term "imprudent"; "innocence" implies the opposite, crime) and in the following sentences ("insufficient surveillance," "caught in the act") link this passage in tone to the highly dramatic "Entry of the Mediums." Breton, who writes in such a lofty and elegant fashion himself, cares desperately about language: it is worth a certain amount of dramatic emphasis.

Words are the most effective creators of energy. They command thought itself, to which they give all its momentum. To the word plays at which Desnos excelled when "asleep," no trivial sense should be assigned; the essay ends with the celebrated lines:

> And let it be quite understood that when we say "word games," it is our surest reasons for living that are being put into play. Words, furthermore, have finished playing games.
>   Words are making love. (OC I, 286)

Breton's 1922 lecture in Barcelona about the modern spirit, forming the last chapter of Lost Steps, is a monument to self-concern, self-confession, and self-importance—and yet, being a witness to the Surrealist movement about to be born, it is supremely valuable as the document of a moment as well as a mind. It has above all the feel of youth, the hopefulness of something just starting out. It was. Surrealism, I think, began here.

Chapter Four
Manifestos

> This summer the roses are blue; wood is glass.
>
> —*First Manifesto, OC* I, 346

First Manifesto

Even at the outset of the *First Manifesto,* the invocation Breton addresses to the imagination—in which he describes the human as a dreamer (*"ce rêveur définitif"*) and the dream as the center of the *real* Surrealist life—is based on the imagination's *unforgiving* quality: "Beloved imagination, what I cherish above all in you is that you never pardon." Relentless, *entier,* the Surrealist spirit in its great intensity has no room for the ordinary patterns of mediocre life, where it is thought necessary to adapt in order to "get along."

Those who are honestly able to echo Breton's famous credo about the possible reconciliation of the apparently contradictory states of dreams and reality—"I believe in the future resolution of these two states"— have no patience with any *adjustment* between ordinary states or conditions and beliefs. They are firmly rooted in the future and in the space that imagination creates beyond the borders of everyday life. Obviously, Surrealism should not be "treated" like any other literary movement, which has its period of influence between such and such years, in such and such a location. It considers itself to be on a different level from ordinary or traditional concerns, no matter how metaphysical they may be. It is a hand pointing *away* from all that we already know. In this first manifesto, Breton protests the efforts of the human imagination to "bring the unknown back to the known," to reduce all we find difficult to understand to the most easily understood basis; the manifesto ends with the haughty proclamation: "Existence is elsewhere" (*OC* I, 346).

As one would expect, the bourgeois standards of art are found lacking in the same criteria as are the logical standards of thought and expression. Not only are they dull and uninteresting in themselves, but they succeed in reducing all they judge to the same dullness, rendering art constantly satisfactory to the majority who need to be reassured, and therefore abhorrent to the Surrealist revolutionaries. Good taste, as a flattening of the individual instinct, is to be challenged whenever possible: "In the bad taste of my time, I try to go further than anyone else." (It is to be noted here that Breton is never content to go only *as far as* anyone else, which would be an essentially traditional attitude. His choice of bad taste as a provocative gesture would have been substantially undercut by such a willingness to seem, even in a minor way, even in a detail of style, like even a few others.) Good taste is usually thought of as that which does not "stand out"; in contrast, the scenery and objects valued by the Surrealists have an extreme quality, a notable oddness: in the Gothic novel (*"roman noir"*), the scenery of ruins and ruined castles as well as the whole series of mannequins, masks, personal eccentricities, and the like. Many of these show a certain morbid fascination not only with the cruel and the unreal, but with the denial of life and movement. And in fact, it would be interesting from this point of view to compare them with several of Breton's favorite images, such as a locomotive going at full speed suddenly stopped in an overgrown forest, or a group of highly sophisticated machines dropped into water that will paralyze them, both images revealing the same cruelty toward *regular* motion and the same exaltation of the bizarre or enforced cessation of the motion.

Breton eulogizes the *insolite*, or the unexpected, the spontaneously revealed marvelous, in the pattern of repetitions and crescendo that is typical of the most forceful Surrealist statements: "The marvelous is always beautiful, any marvelous is beautiful, nothing but the marvelous is beautiful" (*OC* I, 319). The rarity of the marvelous prevents the rule of "always" from imposing a stifling custom on the "aesthetic" principle: all forms of the marvelous are valuable, including those thought to be hideous or even trivial. The latter is, of course, far harder to accept, since most readers of Breton are familiar enough with nineteenth-century writers to have already encountered and absorbed the theory of the grotesque into their scheme of aesthetic judgment—not so with the trivial. The third part of the repetition, moreover, effectively shuts out all customary definitions of beauty with an uncompromising finality.

His attack on the traditional passages of description in the novel, for which he uses as an example the depiction of a room in Dostoevski's *Crime and Punishment,* depends on a refusal to liken people to other people, that is, to reduce them or to reduce individual experiences and aesthetic judgments to other experiences and judgments, or the emotions of one person to the emotions of another, or even to other emotions of the same individual: "I have too unstable a notion of the continuity of life to equal to my best moments my moments of depression, of weakness" *OC* I, 315). Of course this is tantamount to blatantly advocating a certain separation between art and life, since he would deprive the former of any trace of the "worthless moments" along with the weak and depressing ones. What is unworthy of being crystallized in permanent form will eventually disappear from the perfect Surrealist universe.

Such uncompromising attitudes will raise a later difficulty in the matter of automatic transcription, which Breton emphasizes at this point as the basic process of Surrealism: "Pure psychic automatism by means of which it is hoped to express . . . the real functioning of thought. Dictation of thought, in the absence of any control exerted by reason, outside of all esthetic and moral preoccupation" (*OC* I, 328). Surrealism is an act of faith in the superior reality of certain forms of mental association and of the dream, both understood as totally free of any of the constraints that logic, ethics, or aesthetic judgment usually impose.

Now if the unconscious should happen to dictate a dull, ordinary description of a room closely resembling that described in *Crime and Punishment,* what would be the reaction of the Surrealist? Breton states quite clearly that he believes in the infallibility of his own thought, that "thought is strong, and incapable of being in error." Any weakness it shows is the result of exterior distractions, never of the "interior" inspiration, which is supposed to be so reliable that any stylistically weak sentence in the "dictation" will be immediately balanced by the strength of the sentence following it. Breton finds the appeal of inspiration so overwhelming that he likens it to a drug, calling the "spoken thought" technique (*"la pensée parlée"*) inescapable once one has experienced it. It is impossible to leave Surrealism of one's own accord, exactly as if it were a habit dangerous to acquire. All the statements about Surrealism contribute to this view. Just the image of human beings *soluble* in their thoughts, one of Breton's favorites, is enough to put off the weak-hearted inquirer, whereas the enthusiast of Surrealism will recognize the outrageousness of the image as *the point.*

While it is unquestionably true that in some of the Surrealists experiments, such as the "hypnotic slumbers" (during which Robert Desnos, the most gifted of the sleepers, would assault the others), the high melodrama went a long way, we might sometimes wonder if Breton deliberately accentuated the extreme side of the experiments because he felt himself without it to be somewhat tedious: "as far as I am concerned, I used to be considered as tedious as rain—I still am" (*OC* I, 324). In fact, he takes pains to point out that his elder, Pierre Reverdy, was "at least as tedious" as he is, and in fact lauds the older poet, calling "his passion a large part of his charm. No one was ever more thoughtful, or made you more thoughtful, about the deep wellsprings of poetry than he. Once you knew him, nothing seemed as important as his theses on the image in poetry. Nor has anyone else shown such exemplary detachment toward fate's long ingratitude" (*C,* 30). His own views on the image have their origin in Reverdy's famous description of the image as the "bringing together of two more or less distant realities," whose force depends on the distance between the elements of the image as much as on the *"justesse,"* or appropriateness, of their relationship. It is worth quoting Reverdy's exact words, since much will hang on them. The passage is taken from *Nord-Sud*:

> You don't create an image by comparing (always feebly) two disproportionate realities.
>   On the contrary, you create a strong image, new for the mind, by bringing together without comparing them two distant realities whose relation *only the mind* has grasped.[1]

No, says Breton, the mind has grasped nothing *consciously.* More important still, the strength of the image for Breton depends precisely on the *lack* of *"justesse,"* since for him, the function of the image is in its disorienting power.[2] (Aragon states this also in *The Paris Peasant,* where, it is claimed, everybody can find one image that will totally disorient them in the universe, bestowing dizziness, that best of all Surrealist disorders.) The spark, for Breton, comes from the utter disturbance provoked by the very inappropriateness of the two elements, the difference between them:

> For me, the strongest image is the one with the highest degree of arbitrariness. . . . The value of the image depends on the beauty of the spark that is struck: so it is a function of the difference between the two conductors. When this potential scarcely exists, as in a comparison, there is no spark given off. (*OC* I, 338)

As Marguerite Bonnet points out, at the moment of the *Lost Steps* Breton will denigrate Baudelairean correspondences as a timid and transitional idea to be rejected in favor of the more outlandish images found in the pure imagination. However, ten to fifteen years after, in one of the later essays of *Surrealism and Painting* of 1941, he will once more be placing the human mind and the cosmos in relation in poetic analogy, as he does in the game *"the one in the other"* of 1954, and as he had already done in the 1947 essay "Rising Sign," in favor of the empirical power of poetic analogy seen in a "framework of the senses, even of sensuality."[3]

Yet the *First Manifesto* declares a crucial moment of Surrealist discourse and self-conception. Breton underlines the fact that Reverdy's aesthetic is *a posteriori,* that is, a way of judging images already found instead of discovering new images. Surrealists do not invent images— rather they become aware of the images forcing their way into their consciousness as if they were knocking on a window pane. Surrealist poets will eventually be compared to mediums, but never to craftsmen. In a "state of grace," or perfect receptivity, they receive, without ever contradicting, the orders of the marvelous. (See Breton's "Lettre aux voyantes" of 1925, this "Letter to the Mediums," with its lament for the persons forever "lost" for not having followed these orders as they came.)

The *First Manifesto* is a testimony of wonder and acceptance in the face of the marvelous, accompanied by a declaration of absolute nonconformism in the face of the world. Social man in his waking state is held to be less authentic and more limited than man in his dreaming state; in fact, the waking state can be regarded as a tedious *interference* with the limitless domain of the dream.

Second Manifesto

The *Second Manifesto* carries still further the notion of non-compromise, preferably at the risk of social exclusions: "I insist on being considered a fanatic" (*OC* I, 791n). "The public's approval is to be shunned above all. The public must be forbidden *to enter* if confusion is to be avoided. . . . I DEMAND THE PROFOUND AND GENUINE OCCULTATION OF SURREALISM" (*OC* I, 821). Again the tone is categorical, stubborn: *"I claim," "It is essential," "I demand"* . . . The demand is purposely pushed to the extreme, fortified with terms that banish any possibility of nuance: *"fanatic," "above all," "absolutely."* It is never a question of tactful omission for the purpose of public communication, of Surrealism simply withdrawing to an inner sanctum. Breton deliberately emphasizes the exclusion of the non-Surrealists who *have* to be prevented from entering, who have to have things hidden from them, for whom Surrealism *requires* occultation. One would have thought the *hiding* of Surrealism sufficient, without the use of the terms prevention and occultation. This particular technique, which could be described as an accumulation of intensity, fits the frequent personal portraits of Breton as a leonine figure of powerful attraction, given to extremes of enthusiasm and dismay, somehow living on a different level from ordinary mortals who are less violent in their alternations of mood and judgment. It is partly this intensity of feeling that convinces him (rightly) that he can speak to and be heard by all the young people who *refusent le pli,* that is, who refuse to take the crease of ordinariness, to be molded according to the worn-out ideas of family, country, and religion that it is the Surrealists' purpose to subvert, along with the related ideas of calm and happiness.

Surrealism calls itself the tail of Romanticism, repeatedly denouncing the "stupid illusion" of contentment and harmony; it is a "prehensile" tail, for Surrealism cannot be considered *only* a repetition of a former movement. Persons firmly attached to the bourgeois modes of existence or who care about the place they occupy in the world (and here Breton italicizes the words *dans le monde* to convey his scorn for such an attitude) could not conceivably be alive to the multiplication of short circuits taking place in the Surrealist atmosphere. Surrealism is a "mental situation," a psychological place, (*"lieu mental"*), an activity of the mind—to take a more mobile view—searching for a particular *point de l'esprit* or *point sublime,* from which all the oppositions we live with will no longer be seen as contradictions. Death and life, past and future, real and imaginary, height and depth will communicate. References to a "sublime point" recur in a great deal of Breton's writing, as does the image of the *fil* or connecting thread; both are clear expressions of the constant and solemn quest for an ideal unity behind all the series of dualities of which the Surrealists are so conscious.

Human beings are all trapped in the already known, in the already thought—but as the unknown and the marvelous are allowed to penetrate the supposedly closed world of the known, the *thought* (*le pensé*) will gradually succumb to the *thinkable* (*le pensable*) in a universe at last open to imagination and chance. But when the accepted logical fixity of the known gives way, an abyss of madness opens up beneath. Since there is nothing comfortable about following this road of the marvelous above the abyss, many choose a safer path: as Breton states in both the *Second Manifesto* and later in the *Prolegomena to a Third Manifesto of Surrealism or Not,* this more dangerous road cannot even be protected with railings (*garde-fou*). Such *fixed* protection would be itself a threat to the newly opened universe, which is admittedly a dangerous one. When Breton wishes to praise Picasso, he calls him the artist who places no railing on his bridges; this is a further example of Surrealism's *"integral character,"* its uncompromising intensity. Better to fall into madness (Breton gives a certain value to the fall itself, as he states in connection with *Nadja*) or "to pass through to the other side of the mirror" than not to dare the adventure. Surrealism, after all, exists to see and to show "the other side of the real," and one can scarcely expect that to be a trivial vision.

Nor can the *means* of vision be trivial. Breton compares the Surrealists' attitude toward their work with that of the alchemists—the value of the philosopher's stone was that it permitted the "dazzling revenge" of the human imagination on everything else. He takes Rimbaud's term *l'alchimie du verbe* in its fullest sense, the Word being the model for the human soul, the omnipresent mover of the universe: "thus it is as much in what we fear as in what we write, as in what we love." In opposition to all the dulling categories of ordinary life, the Surrealist pushes against the limits of the human mind. The *Second Manifesto* ends with an eloquent invocation of mental adventure, which takes fully into account the possibility of failure and determines to count even that a victory:

> Let him use in spite of all prohibitions, the avenging weapon of the *idea* against the bestiality of all beings and of all things; and then one day when he is vanquished—but vanquished only if the *world is world*—let him greet the firing of the sad guns as if it were a salute. (*OC* I, 828)

Prolegomena to a Third Manifesto of Surrealism or Not

The *Prolegomena to a Third Manifesto of Surrealism or Not* begins with Breton's disclaimer of a total adhesion to any system; he explains that there is too much of the northerner in him for that, too much "granite" and "fog." As a balance to the hope and pride represented by the possibility of a *sublime point,* he discerns the possibility of a *fallible point* in all the theories he has held. No system of principles is perfect, even alone or in its ideal state, and in combination with human fallibility, the imperfect is aggravated; "perhaps every great idea is liable to serious alteration the moment it comes in contact with the mass of men, where it is forced to compromise with minds of a different temper than those from which it sprang" (*Manifestos,* 338).[4] There follows a negative catalog: "As long as men have not become conscious of their condition . . . , it is not worth talking . . . it is still less worth loving . . . it is still less worth dying and . . . still less worth living." But directly preceding the last factor of this series is a lyrical parenthesis: "I always think of youth, of the trees *in*

bloom in New York," which is echoed by the next sentence, *"There is,* I
think of that beautiful optimistic formula of gratitude which recurs in
Apollinaire's last poems . . ." (340). This is the beginning of a totally
positive catalog balancing the negative one as the consciousness of a fallible point balances that of a sublime one—the style and the temper of
Surrealism are to a great extent determined by the play of dualities and
their alternating resolution and redivision.

And then Breton moves from the statement of the marvelous (*"Il y
a": there is*) to the demands of humanism (*"Il faut": there must be*). Human
beings must no longer be exploited by their fellows, or by the "absurd
and provocative idea" of God. The idea of love must also be reexamined,
and finally, human beings must put themselves, forever and firmly, on
the human side. The passage builds up to a final series of impatient
protests: "Enough weakness, enough childishness . . . enough flowers on
graves, enough civic instruction between two classes of gym, enough tol-
erance, enough serpents!" (341). The *opposition* must be strengthened;
men must be convinced that when "everyone" has agreed on a thing, the
only way out of the imprisoning *likeness* of belief is an individual resistance to the common perception. Breton calls the latter the only key to
the fields—thus, his subsequent title. He claims as the goal of his voyage, on which he invites us, "the opening of windows" on the greatest
"utopian landscapes."

All Dada and Surrealist manifestations are manifestos of liberation.
When we accept those principles, this exploration of our own subcon-
scious is supposed to free us from the constraints of society and art; when
we commit ourselves to the Surrealist principles, it is not as if this were
to be another reassuring category: Breton states plainly that there can be
too much conformism even among the Surrealists. Surrealism is to be a
continuing scandal (corresponding to the "scandal of the world") and a
personal risk, or it will not be.

Chapter Five
1928: Nadja

Who am I?

Again, I prefer walking in the night to believing myself to be walking in the daylight.

Nadja, OC I, 647

In *Surrealism and Painting,* Breton represents the painter André Derain (who was original enough to concern himself, for instance, not with the weight of the glass of water upon the table, but with the pressure of the table upward on the glass) as reproducing a definite *"modern disturbance."* The opening line of *Nadja,* "Who am I?" can be taken just as easily for an example of the disturbed mind, because it leads directly to another question, "Whom do I haunt?" the word "haunt" revealing between the author and certain other beings "relationships more singular, less avoidable, more troubling than I would have thought." One of the first things to point out about the book is that the photographs here, and in *Communicating Vessels* and *Mad Love,* link these three works inextricably, as they were meant to be linked. They are all testimonies to the difference between simply documenting life and living it in a higher register; they are an exaltation of its energies, as they are all examinations of *hauntings.*[1]

In spite of the title, the initial and indeed the principal subject of the book is not Nadja's search for self-identity, but Breton's. Nadja, whose name is the beginning of the Russian word for hope (and only the beginning), does not enter the book until after the first third of the text, and she fades out of it in the last part. She is important only as a stage in Breton's autobiography, as an example of the possible genius of the mentally abnormal and of their inexcusable treatment in "asylums," and as a contrast with the more "adaptable" behavior of the author and his friends. She troubles his mind temporarily, but she can in no way affect his general comportment or his permanent sentiments. This is a pitifully one-sided love story; Nadja, who loves Breton as "the sun," is finally found by him to be less interesting than the more "normal" woman to whom the end of the book is addressed.

As for Nadja herself, she is described as being of an utter "fragility, with an imperceptible smile, and her makeup only half applied." The letter she leaves under André Breton's door when she realizes that their affair is ending could scarcely be more moving:

> "Thank you, André," she writes, "I have had everything from you . . . I don't want to take any more of your time from the superior things you should do. —Everything you do will be well done—Let nothing stop you—There are already enough people who have as their mission the extinction of the Fire—It is wiser not to dwell on the impossible. . . . Nadja." (*OC* I, 1513)

Breton undertakes the book, then, not as a testimonial to the extraordinary character whose name it bears, but as an inquiry into what is individual about himself. What part of his personality continues through all the events he experiences, all the gestures he makes, and in the unique tastes he recognizes himself as having, and how does this individuality separate him from others? It is scarcely necessary to point out that Nadja's separation from the mass of human beings is in some less drastic way paralleled by Breton's. As if one had asked "Why should one go to any length to discover one's own difference?" Breton answers:

> Isn't it true that in the extent to which I become conscious of this differentiation I shall find out what I came to do in this world among all the other people and of what unique message I am the bearer, answering for it with my life? (*OC* I, 648)

But he refuses to consider this exploration of his life a return upon his footsteps (like the image of a ghost conjured up by the expression "haunt"), because the footsteps are in no way lost. Nor are those of the first book of essays unambiguously lost, since *Les Pas perdus,* or the *Lost Steps,* sometimes translated as *Wandering Steps,* might be read as meaning "What Is Not Lost" as well. The title, of course, has to do with waiting rooms in train stations, those perfect places for Surrealist encounters.

All the ideas connected with Christianity, like loss, the fall, penance, are totally opposed by the Surrealist way of thought, which confers upon the same terms a contrary sense. So is the idea of an author's deliberate mystification: it is essential to know the way in which anyone looks at certain things. Authors have no right to hide the key to their books, to surround their characters with superficial mystery, changing the color of the heroine's hair from blonde to brunette so as to protect the real woman behind the story. For Breton, the only interesting works are left ajar like doors and can be entered by anyone:

> As for me, I shall continue to inhabit my glass house, where anyone coming to visit me can be seen at any hour . . . where I rest at night on a glass bed with glass sheets, where *what I am* will appear to me sooner or later traced with a diamond. (*OC* I, 651)[2]

Events will not be covered over with a polite façade—for his own attitude toward Nadja, which may seem heartless to the reader, he will make no excuses.

The entry for the eleventh of October betrays a complete lack of sensitivity: "What is more, Nadja arrived late and I do not expect from her anything exceptional. We wander along the streets, near each other, but very separate. . . . It is aggravating to see her reading the menus on restaurant doors and juggling the names of certain dishes. I am bored" (*OC* I, 710). Whether such intensity is here, or is always, compensated for by equal sincerity is not the sort of judgment a Surrealist or his reader is asked to make, falling as it does within the realm of standard ethical questions and therefore outside the Surrealist realm, which is nothing if not nonstandard.

The lack of order in this "novel" is planned. Breton will in all cases prefer chance to orderly calculation, the "caprice of the moment" to a preconceived system. His purpose is to relate only

> [t]he most significant episodes of my life *such as I conceive it outside of its organic design,* that is in the extent to which it is subjugated to chance happenings, to the smallest as to the greatest, where protesting against the usual idea I have of it, it introduces me into a sort of forbidden world of sudden relationships, petrifying coincidences, of reflexes taking the lead over any mental reaction, of chords struck as on the piano, of sparks that one could see by, but really *see,* if they were not even more rapid than the others. (*OC* I, 651)

Certain facts or observations take on the appearance of *signals,* even when one is not sure what they are designating; rather than confusing them with the mass of ordinary facts, Breton simply suppresses the latter—hence the odd atmosphere of the work. Even among the significant facts, there is as great a range as between totally "automatic" texts that come freely and the "reflective" ones, for which the author bears the responsibility. (It is obvious that Breton is averse to arrangements, distinctions, and "ordering" only insofar as they represent a logic he finds imprisoning.) He says of the signal-facts:

> These facts could be ranked in a hierarchy from the simplest to the most complex, from the special, indefinable movement provoked by the sight of some unusual objects[3] or by our arrival in such and such a place, accompanied by the very clear sensation that for us something serious, something essential is involved, to the complete inability to be at peace with ourselves produced by certain trains of events, certain groups of circumstances which go far beyond our understanding, and, in most cases, permit no return to a rational activity unless we call on our instinct of conservation. A great quantity of intermediate steps could be set up between those "faits-glissades"—those facts you slide into—and these "faits-précipices"—or the facts that send you plunging. (*OC* I, 652)

The images from which the last two terms are derived indicate Breton's attitude toward "real" experiences: they are most valuable to him when they lead away from themselves to a set of "irrational" feelings and actions, and the more directly they lead away, the more valuable they are. The *"precipice"* or cliff over which one is bound to fall unless preserved by the life instinct is to be infinitely preferred to the *"glissade"* or slope which one could, if overtaken by panic, reascend by means of one's own resources of intelligence. Surrealism places a higher value on risk than on safety, on intensity than on reasonableness or intellect. The facts to which one is only the "haggard witness" take precedence over those whose details and outcomes are easily discerned, so by implication it is better to be forced to look than to see voluntarily. The structure of *Nadja,* insofar as it needs or finds justification, functions only as a support for these facts, and has no more cohesion than they do. Possibly *Nadja* itself could function as a *"fait-glissade"* (and for some sensitive readers, even a *"fait-précipice"*), since created works serve as experiences, and since in fact Breton does say he writes in the effort to provoke the same sorts of sensations he has experienced. An honest recognition of the ability to find pride and even pleasure in the danger implied by the images of sliding and falling, although it is not by any means confined to Surrealist psychology, is essential to the understanding of all Surrealist work and of the power of such an image as the removal of guardrails from the bridges over the precipice.

In all these respects, *Nadja* serves as an indispensable introduction to the theory of Surrealism. There are variations, of course, as the movement develops, perhaps the most obvious being the attitude toward automatic writing and the degree of the author's responsibility: Breton will eventually regret that so much importance was attached to it, claiming that in fact the mind was always to some extent the director of the hand. But in 1963 when he reedits *Nadja*, the changes are not major ones, except for his notes, in which he reinterprets the original text: "Surrealism was still looking for itself," he will say. He insists, in the introduction to the new edition, on its "antiliterary" quality; the abundant photographic illustration intends to eliminate all descriptions (attacked in the *First Manifesto*), while the tone of medical observation intends to undermine the notion of literary style in favor of a spontaneous document. Breton believes the purposely bare style of *Nadja*, its *"dénouement volontaire,"* to be largely responsible for its wide audience, since this very lack of ornamentation enables its vanishing point (*"point de fuite"*) to recede far beyond the ordinary limits of vision. Like the images of slope and precipice, that of flight indicates movement from one level or location to another. Motion is a constant of Surrealist thought and theory, and Nadja, the wandering soul, is perhaps the perfect Surrealist.

Breton describes, in no particular order, a series of unusual objects and the unusual sensations or realizations that *necessarily* accompany them: a copy of Rimbaud with other poems inserted, one blue glove of surprising weight, as if it were pressing on another hand, and the optical illusion of a sign that reads "Maison Rouge" and seems from another angle to read "Police," representing by coincidence the repressive authorities and connected by irrational but "inevitable" circumstances to the illusion of a picture representing a tiger or a vase or an angel, depending on the angle of vision. Thus he means to reveal the impossibility or "at least the grave insufficiency" of any so-called rigorous calculation of the notion of personality and the motives for our actions. This, he hopes, will send a number of people into the streets, the street being the obvious place for chance encounters, where mystery can easily prevail over calculations of all sorts, and where sudden attractions,[4] ambiguous situations, and reversals of attitude abound. Nadja herself is the "always inspired and inspiring creature who only liked to be in the street, for her the only place of valid experience, in the street in reach of the questions of all human beings who have thrown themselves into a great chimerical question" (*OC* I, 716).

Breton places a great value on any situation that potentially disturbs his mental habits. The ideal one he gives as an example, of meeting a beautiful naked woman in the forest, is not only unlikely but no longer

meaningful once he has expressed the desire (because it would then leave
the realm of the spontaneous for that of the predicted); however, his
brief discussion of the example is particularly interesting.

> It seems to me that *everything* would have stopped short, ah! I wouldn't
> be writing what I am writing. I adore this situation in which more than
> in any other I would probably have lost my *presence of mind*. I would not
> have even had enough to flee. (Those who laugh at this last sentence are
> pigs.) (34)

This would, without question, be a *"fait-précipice,"* and yet Breton uses
not an image of falling, but of stopping. If he had the presence of mind
to call on his instinct of conservation, he would be able to move, yet he
does not. At the height of Surrealist adventure, then, there is a sudden
cessation of the motion which has led up to it; at one point in
Communicating Vessels Breton recommends retreat to the calm center of
the tornado.

Nadja's entire life, she admits, consists of telling herself stories, and
Breton comments that this sort of life is the extreme limit of Surrealist
aspiration. Nevertheless, directly after this admission, when Breton asks
her where she will go upon leaving him at his door, she remarks how
easy it is to begin by going back to the place where they were. It is precisely as if there were no idea of progress at all on the personal level, as if
all the references to "one day" and "there will be" referred only to communication or liberation in the social realm.

The famous definition at the end of the book—"Beauty will be CON-
VULSIVE or will not be"—might lead one to suppose that the Surrealist
"aesthetic" was based only on movement. But the preceding paragraphs
are indispensable to its comprehension. Breton has insisted that beauty
is neither completely dynamic nor completely static: "It is like a train
that starts up in the Lyon station when I know it is never going to leave,
that it has not left. It is made of jolts [*"saccades"*] many of which have
scarcely any importance but we know they bring on a final *Jolt* which has
enormous importance" (*OC* I, 753). This image should be considered in
connection with another which is its exact reverse, that is, the speeding
train stopped in the forest. Breton wants to indicate in this passage "the
exact expiration of this movement" as well as the "relationship linking
the object in its movement and in its repose." Like the image of the communicating vessels of reality and surreality, these last images are combi-
nations of opposites, whose resolution is *never a reduction* and never a
simplification.

"It is possible that this desperate chase will stop here? Chase after what, I do not know, but *chase,* to bring into play all the artifices of mental seduction" (*OC* I, 714). Breton has by now traced all the elements composing his *"lumière propre,"* the particular lighting in which his nature is best visible. And here he places the mystery of Nadja's personality, which is in so many other places considered antipathetic to his, in close conjunction with his own. Instead of "Who am I?" we now hear the question:

> Who were we in front of reality, this reality which I now perceive curled up at Nadja's feet like a naughty dog? . . . How did it come about that projected together once and for all so far from the earth, we were able in the brief intervals which our marvelous stupor accorded us, to exchange a few looks of incredible agreement above the smoking remains of the old thought and this neverceasing life? (*OC* I, 714)

But even if Breton considers reality to be subjected to Nadja's power, he is totally unable to share for any sustained period of time in her purely intuitive and detached way of conducting herself in the everyday world where he feels himself forced to live. She is beyond it and irremediably beyond him, neither listening to his words nor noticing his boredom, and so he feels himself incapable of helping her resolve her many difficulties "normally." Whether we are intended to concentrate on the irony latent in the latter expression is unclear. In any case, the split between Nadja's feelings and those of Breton is pitifully clear, and it is disturbing on all sides. As we have seen, Breton always makes a sharp distinction between what is valuable and what is not, from his—that is, the Surrealist—viewpoint; Nadja, on the other hand, does not judge between moments, does not separate them according to their interest:

> I had, long since, ceased to get along with Nadja very well. To tell the truth, perhaps we never agreed, at least on the manner of looking at the simple things of existence. She had chosen once and for all not to pay any attention, not to care about the hour, not to make any distinction between the idle talk she sometimes made and the other kind that mattered so much to me, not to take any notice of my passing moods and of the more or less serious difficulty I had in pardoning her worst distractions. (*OC* I, 735)

While she narrates the details of "the most lamentable" circumstances of her life, Breton is "reduced to waiting, with a frown," for her to move on to something else. (Needless to say, it is not a question of their moving together toward something else.) Breton is accustomed to accepting the passive role in the face of the marvelous, but he demands that the marvelous be *constantly* marvelous. He describes Nadja's drawings, he gives us Nadja's drawings, and finally, he is bored by them. He cannot accept her being either "natural" or unnatural, like or unlike other women, and it is because she is not perpetually interesting in what he calls her "exercises" that she cannot be forgiven. In fact, the "exercises" that Eluard and Breton did together of mental aberrations, that is, their imitations of the style of those aberrations, are beautiful, and they *are* interesting. *L'Immaculée conception* (the title they give to these exercises) is never as dull as Nadja seems to Breton, but then it is the work of two poets.

Nadja, Breton says, does not have a "real conception of her value. . . ." If he had only loved her, in the sense he means love ("mysterious, improbable, unique, confusing and indubitable"), he would have been content to accept her in her differences from him. Surrealist love is spontaneous and cannot be chosen. It was not given to Breton to love Nadja:

> Everything that enables a person to live on the simple life of another, without ever wanting to obtain from him more than he gives, that makes it sufficient just to see him moving or still, speaking or silent, waking or asleep, did not exist, had never existed: that was only too certain. It could not have been otherwise, considering Nadja's world, where everything so quickly took on the appearance of rising and falling. But I am judging *a posteriori* and I am taking a risk in saying it could never be otherwise. Whatever might have been my desire, or possibly my illusion, I was not up to what she suggested to me. (*OC* I, 735–36)

The blank space left in the text between the paragraph where Breton admits his possible shortcomings, a paragraph that ends with a construction patently contrary to fact: "only love . . . could have permitted in this case the bringing about of the miracle," and the beginning of the next paragraph is in itself tragic. Without that miracle, there can never be communication between the "normal" world and the other, even for a Surrealist—"They came, some months ago, to tell me that Nadja was insane" (*OC* I, 736).

Nadja, unlike the "normal" Surrealists, has no instinct to call herself back from the precipice, does not know how to comport herself:

> Now I never imagined that she might lose or might already have lost the *help* of that instinct of conservation—to which I have already referred—

and which means that, after all, my friends and I *behave ourselves,* for example, when a flag passes—limiting our action to turning our heads away. (*OC* I, 741)

For those who "pass to the other side of the mirror" Breton has a genuine respect—which does not prevent him from remaining on this side. Nadja's conception of the proof of love was to rush headlong to their death together, with Breton at the wheel of the car, blinded by her hands over his eyes. She was capable of a *total* subversion of the life instinct, and although in retrospect Breton admits the validity of such a test for friendship and for love ("Ideally at least I often find myself blindfolded at the wheel of this wild car," [44]), it is undeniable that at this time he refused it. Would he have accepted, being in love?

The question at the end of this section—"Who goes there?"—is posed by Breton to himself, and he calls it an "always pathetic" cry. "Who goes there? Is it you, Nadja? Is it true that the *beyond* is in this life? I cannot hear you. Who goes there? Is it only I? Is it myself?" (*OC* I, 743). The book could have ended with this question as the only echo for the opening question; Nadja could have been only an exteriorization of the risk of Surrealism, made explicit and then eliminated. Yet in the last few pages, Breton begins again, not with a self-questioning but with an affirmation of the Surrealist manner of living life breathlessly, with a new sense of every moment, even those between the printed words in a sentence.

Every sentiment here is turned to the positive, so that the silence is no longer seen, like the space between two worlds and the two paragraphs just mentioned, as a solitude, but as a space for miraculous change, from "myself" to the next "present sense of myself." Breton repeats the Surrealist credo in the unconscious, in uncertainty, in impatience, and in risk, as a balance (deliberate or unconscious?) for the more conservative passages on social behavior:

> Nonetheless if one has to wait, to wish for certainty, to take precautions, to clear a particular space for the fire and only a particular space,[5] I refuse completely. Let the great unconscious, in all its vitality and reverberation, the unconscious which inspires my only convincing acts, dispose forever of all that I am. I remove from myself for no reason any opportunity to take back what I am once again granting. (*OC* I, 749)

The strength of this *irrational* vow and imprudent behavior compensates for whatever timidity and reserve we might have sensed in the comparison between Breton and Nadja, a comparison that he was at least honest enough to make.

However we may feel about Nadja's final replacement by the next incarnation of the free spirit (*"génie libre"*), we cannot deny that the ending is a strong one, as the woman loved gives to the already determined conclusion about the convulsive beauty its "true sense and all its force." Breton affirms his faith in the uniqueness of love as it puts an end to all the puzzling self-examinations ("Who am I?") and to the anguish of solitude ("Is it only I?"):

> All I know is that the substitution of persons stops with you, because nothing can be substituted for you, and that for me this succession of enigmas was always destined to stop in front of you.
>
> You are not an enigma for me.
>
> I say that you turn me away forever from the enigma. (*OC* I, 752)

This last gesture Nadja could never have made. She was herself the mystery and pointed only to the mystery. That Breton should have preferred the non-enigma or the transcendence of enigma to the embodiment of enigma is perhaps not surprising from a human viewpoint, even if one would have drawn other conclusions from the precepts of Surrealism. Not only is it a great proof of humility, but it incorporates the ironies and the dualities that give to Surrealism its characteristic tone.

After all his self-examination, Breton concludes that the final *saccade* of beauty has all the importance that he would rather not give to himself. And after all the lyricism of language and the "marvelous" of anecdotes and strange events, he invokes their opposites: "Kingdom of silence . . ." Parallel to the image of the self-destructive couple in the car, the final image of the plane with which all communication is cut off is an example perhaps of convulsive beauty, and certainly of enigma. We may suspect that the plane does not crash and that the pilot is accompanied (Breton having said that the woman by his side in the car could have been any other as well as Nadja, and even a "certain other person"), but we cannot be sure. There is just as much distance between us and the plane as there was between Breton and the insane asylum, and perhaps this distance still remains between him and the pilot. "A morning newspaper will always suffice to bring me news of myself" (*OC* I, 753), which is entirely as it should be in a Surrealist novel. Any questions asked at the end are finally as much ours as they are the author's.

Chapter Six
1932: Communicating Vessels

Now that I no longer look for her, I happen to meet her sometimes. Her eyes are still just as
beautiful, but I have to admit that she has lost her specialness for me.

—Communicating Vessels, VC, 82

Surrealism, in Breton's view, is primarily a unifying force. Against all
separations and specializations it poses its single most important visual
image, the communicating vessels already perceived in the first version
of *Surrealism and Painting* of 1928. The volume that takes the name of
the image is an indispensable document about linkings—of elements
with each other—and connections—as well as differences—between
Surrealism and Marxist theory.

Central to the book is a definition of Surrealism far more wide-
reaching than the often quoted definition in the *First Manifesto* about
automatism:

> I hope it will be seen as having tried nothing better than to lay down a
> *conduction wire* between the far too distant worlds of waking and sleep,
> exterior and interior reality, reason and madness, the assurance of knowl-
> edge and of love, of life for life and the revolution, and so on. (*VC*, 86)[1]

And then, since this is a defense of Surrealism against the accusation
of its nonparticipation in the social revolution, Breton adds with characteristic feeling:

> At least it will have tried, perhaps inefficaciously, but tried, to leave no
> question without an answer and to have cared a little about the coherence
> of the answers given. Supposing that this terrain was ours, did it really
> deserve to be abandoned? (*VC*, 86)

Divided into three parts, the book does not give the same impression
of willed disorder as *Nadja*. In the first part, Breton makes an ingenious
and even convincing case for linking imagination to action, and the time
and space of the dream to that of the material world. In the second, he
illustrates by personal experiences the workings of objective chance and

the place of human love in the revolution against the bourgeois world as it stands. And in the third, he discusses the future relationship of the individual poet to the revolution and to other people.

The fact that *Communicating Vessels* has a slightly more "ordered" form does not invalidate the image of the swinging door found in *Nadja*. Here Breton only modifies that image to make it a half-open door between the imagined and the lived "or, more exactly, the ought-to-live," so that it takes just one step to leave the "shaky house of poets and to find one-self on a level with life itself."

It has so far, says Breton, not been to the advantage of "literary people" to investigate the relationship between the two worlds, because they have claimed, although wrongfully, the revelations of dream as their property. What is worse, they have exalted dream over action as a social-ly conservative device, since those who would be tempted to make revo-lutions can be persuaded instead to dream: this keeps them out of action's way. As for the professional psychologists (they practice the "*last* of the sciences") who should have taken a more responsible position, they have simply pushed "to the new shore, with beetle-like gestures, the ball of not very pertinent opinions that they have been rolling in front of them from the beginning of time" (15). There is even a danger that the dream enigma be turned by some of them into the "most cre-tinizing religious mystery."

From the standpoint of its emphatically antireligious position as well as its insistence on the abolition of any separation between "specializa-tions," Surrealism is most decidedly humanistic. All the beginning pages of this volume lead up to the statement in the final part that the human being is the center of the universe and the only possible location for the resolution of its contradictions. For the Surrealists, belief in God and the future life is an obvious reduction of the importance of the human imag-ination and its full creative power within this present life, which must be changed rather than transcended. So far the commentators on dream have neglected to indicate "on which side of the barricade they put themselves." Freud himself did not go far enough in his conclusions, since he separated "psychic reality" from "material reality," refused the prophetic dream dealing with the immediate future, and did not apply the full extent of his investigations to his own case. Breton calls this a *desertion* like any other.

The lengthy interpretation of his own dreams that follows in the first part (using Freud's method of interpretation) is to be seen as an example of the continuous mental activity taking place during sleep. The second part, opening with Breton recounting his dreams to Eluard, who serves as the listener in these psychoanalytic sessions[2], contains a long account of Breton's daily life, oneiric in its structure, illogical but marvelous in atmosphere:

> No sooner is one character seen than he is dropped for another—and, who knows, even for another? So then what is the point of all this exposition? The author seemed to be telling us something about his life, but he speaks as if in a dream! *As if in a dream.* (*VC,* 75)[3]

The autobiographical analysis here is the exact counterpart of the dramatic analysis in the first part: a series of coincidences accompanied by commentaries on sentences that come spontaneously to mind. The chance links and recurrences (for example, of the names Olga, Samson, Batifol, etc.) exemplify the Surrealist belief in objective chance, similar to the theory of Engels that Breton quotes: "Causality can not be understood except as it is linked with the category of objective chance, a particular form of the manifestation of necessity" (*VC,* 92). In all of this there are two conclusions implied. First, that the structure of the dream and of reality closely resemble each other, the marvelous and the human mind functioning alike. Second, that love is an agent of perfection and of knowledge as well as of madness, working against idealization, progressing toward whatever is more specific.

On the purely choreographic level, the intertwining of the communicating vessels into the "unity of the materialist world" balances the recurring stress on Breton's position, in fact, his *disposition* of solitude, the split between his experiences with the marvelous, these realizations of coincidence, and his observations of "average" life ("solid, not very productive, but at least unarguable," 84). The Sunday crowds by the river could never share the intensely charged atmosphere of drama he inhabits:

> I imagined without the slightest irony everything that could be indissoluble, easy between them. Two by two, they had chosen each other, one day just like that, and there had no longer been any question of their being able to leave each other. No afterthought, finally, on either side. . . . The need to understand the world a little, the desire to be different from others, the hope of helping some situation not quite resolved to resolve itself—all this kind of thing at once exciting and disappointing would never come up at all. All the same, it is for those people that there are strawberries in the woods! (*VC,* 83–84)

While affirming that it is too late for him to resemble them in any way, Breton thinks their position a privileged one "up to a certain point." Read rapidly, this seems a sort of colonialist posture—the natives have their advantages, too, the simple life is tempting, but on another level from ours, and so on. The isolated hero ("I repeat I was alone") expresses a genuine modesty about the human situation in which he participates: How can one manage to be simply an individual, with no particular claim to anything beyond? To justify the "room one takes up in eating, drinking, dressing, sleeping" by intellectual accomplishments[4] is far more difficult than to do so by physical labor. The clear appeal of the primitive remains strong. The intellectual comradeship Breton so often underlines (*"my friends and I"*) takes the place of that communication of spirit in the Sunday crowds of couples. Ideally it should fill in the rift between Breton and those whose destiny is different, easier, as the rift between the two conceptions of Revolution is ideally resolved at the end of the book when outside communicates with inside, poets with "the others," light with dark, and dream with reality.

Breton's goal in this book is plainly one of resolution, of uniting what is now separate. The dream must be replaced "in its true framework, which could only be human life itself" (*VC*, 17), showing that the supposed split between conscious thought and "total repose" is not only illusory but harmful. The exile of the imagining person into an unconscious every night leads to a dangerous spiritualization of consciousness. Although the dream is a potential liberating force, mystifications antipathetical to the free spirit easily attach to it.

In the first and third parts of the book, the major theme of the connection between dream and reality recurs in various formulations, accompanied by various images. The most successful of the latter is probably that of the *capillary tissue* lying between the two realms, assuring a constant interchange between the exterior and interior worlds, objective knowledge and subjective sentiment, the waking and the sleeping being. The human being mediates, says Breton, between two worlds, resolving all contradictions in a "universal subjectivity." The general aim of Surrealism, as Breton now states it, is to go beyond the simple joining of elements to each other, which was its starting point and continues to determine its aesthetics and its stylistics, in order to modify the human role. Surrealism intends "to replace human beings at the heart of the universe, to take them away for a second from the disintegrating adventure, reminding them that they are for all the sadness and joy exterior to themselves an infinitely perfectible place of resolution and echo" (*VC*, 147). While objective knowledge is likely to teach cynicism, desire refuses itself nothing. "Resignation is not written on the moving stone of sleep" (*VC*, 145).

Not only does the *"pur décor"* of the exterior world cut off all the imaginative realities and the countless possibilities glimpsed in the world of sleep, but its temporal structure makes slaves of us, as we plunge into "the search for concrete, continuous, immediate efficacity. . . . This time I live in, this time, alas, runs by and takes me with it" (*VC*, 135). One has here not so much the sense of Surrealist longing for an atemporal paradise as an actual impatience with the present moment. Breton feels it significant that the cloud of his particular epoch "should draw its shadow over the page I am writing on, that this tribute should be paid to the plurality in which, in order to dare to write, I must at once lose and find myself" (*VC*, 135). Only beyond the shadow of this cloud, representing the economic regime of capitalism, can a person presume to give play to more individual feelings. In short, the impatience can be defined as wanting to "hasten the hour of the Revolution," when the human mind, freed from its more ignoble material wants, will be "raised to a higher level" (*VC*, 136).

And here the split between Surrealist thinking and traditional Marxist thinking is clarified, or better, illuminated in its own ambiguity. The shadow cast on the page once acknowledged, the faith in a permanent revolution once stated, the subject of the verb "write" emerges as more important than it might have seemed before. Breton has justified the study of a self only in terms of "being able to integrate it with the collective being," but after losing itself in the plurality of voices, the individual voice finds itself once more stronger than they are:

> Perhaps it is fitting that there should be shaped, in the most tormented periods and even against their will, the solitude of a few whose role is to preserve in some corner of a hothouse what can not have any but a fleeting existence, in order to find much later its place in the center of a new order, thus marking with a flower that is absolutely and simply present, because it is *true*—a flower in some way *axial in relation to time*—that tomorrow should be linked all the more closely with yesterday for having to break off in a more decisive manner with it? (*VC*, 138)

Breton wills himself a revolutionary, but he cannot will himself one of the present masses. He calls for action, but it is to some extent circumscribed within the realm of magic "in that it consists of an unconscious, immediate action of the internal on the external and that there easily enters into the summary analysis of such a notion the idea of a transcendental mediation which is probably rather that of a demon than that of a god" (*VC,* 147).

Yet the most interesting sorts of ambiguity are revealed not in the content, but rather in the style. Magic may be considered an "immediate" action, but the final passage of the book is in the lyric future, the privileged tense of the Surrealists, who often substitute for Apollinaire's *"il y a"* or THERE IS an *"il y aura"* or THERE WILL BE. "The poet to come will surmount the depressing idea of the irreparable divorce between action and dream" (*VC,* 146). Breton is not describing, nor could he describe, the poetic work at the moment when he pictures its final emergence into broad daylight. When the "hair streaming with light" that he attributes to truth appears at the "dark window," uniting the brightness and the shadow, the poets will have gone outside to mingle with the others. The writer, like the reader, is swept beyond the cloud, into a state of pure lyricism.

Beside all the other ambiguities felt in Breton's work, there is this most tragic one that seems to predominate over all the rest: *Surrealist poetry wills itself present, but its entire feeling is future.* It is never quite here. The constant refusal to foresee an *end* to revolution is not just a theoretical refusal, it is also a temperamental one. The declaration at the beginning of *Communicating Vessels* about "those who have judged once and for all that after so many interpretations of the world it is time to pass to its transformation" (*VC,* 10) places only the passing over in the present moment; the transformation is marked as belonging to the continuous future. Some may consider this split between the poets of the present and their vision of the future to be a final, unconscious alienation of being from action, of vision from reality, and a confirmation of the tenuous quality of the communication between vessels of any sort. The perspective from which the reader will consider this particular text depends, perhaps more than any other of Breton's texts, on the distance acknowledged between poetry and life. Breton himself increasingly considered any such acknowledgment a compromise—it is in the light of his uncompromising attitude that the text takes on its full tragic and heroic depth.

> There is today, it is true, little room for anyone who would haughtily trace in the grass the learned arabesques of the suns. . . . (*VC,* 135)

Chapter Seven
1934: Break of Day

Nothing, it seems to me, is inadmissible . . . Latin civilization has had its day and I, for one, ask that it not be saved . . . Let others be attached to their family, their country, and the land, I am a stranger to that kind of emulation. I have only loved in myself what seemed to be in greatest contrast with the outside, and I've never been in the slightest bothered about my interior equilibrium.[1]

The essays grouped under the title "Break of Day" include the major themes and theories of Surrealism, which can be placed in three general divisions—first, the role of language as a determiner of the world; second, the value of the unknown in contrast to the known, and of the multiple and equivocal in contrast to the simple; and finally, the connection between a certain contemporary state of unrest common to human beings and things, on one hand, and the miraculous revelation of a new "crystalline" reality, on the other. The themes are at once inextricably linked and inseparable, both developing and unchanging over the decade covered in the essays, as is appropriate to the always paradoxical nature of Surrealism.

Reality and the Seer

The "reality" in the difficult title "Introduction au Discours sur le peu de réalité" is seen as sparse in quantity, or minor in power, in relation to the power of the human imagination and its weapon, the word. In this sense, the essay with this title, which opens the collection, is a continuation of the essay "Les Mots sans rides," those fresh, young, unwrinkled words of Lost Steps. Since, for Breton, the individual mind, through its language and living power, is able to control much of the world, we have to devise all possible ways to rearrange its composition incessantly. Immobility is fatal to new thoughts and patterns. In the vitalizing of the world our most effective tool is language: what we say controls even what we are able to see.

"Doesn't the mediocrity of our universe depend essentially on our power of enunciation?" (OC II, 276). If we permit our words always to be reassembled in their ordinary ways, we are necessarily accepting the unchanging aspect of things as they have always appeared to us. "Words tend to group themselves according to particular affinities, which generally work to recreate the world in every moment just like the old model" (*OC* II, 275); there can be no new vision without a new tongue.

The most frequent and the gravest mistake nonpoets make is to "translate" poetic images into common terms under the excuse of explaining them, a process which immediately does away with all their potentially generative force. Against someone who tries to explain that the poet Saint-Pol Roux's image of the "crystal breast" really means a carafe or a vase, Breton unleashes a righteous anger. Be sure, he says, the poet Saint-Pol Roux said what he meant to say. One image does not *mean* another, and anyone who tries to facilitate the task of the reader is actually reducing the priceless complexity of the human imagination. Why *must* we always flatten things out, why this fear of pluralism? Our love of simplicity leads us to formulate easy categories; when we put things in a placid and satisfactory order, we are denying their capacity for multiplicity and movement, and our own flexibility and range of vision. Surrealism demands always the most complete experience, and often it insists that this experience be shared by the greatest number.[2]

"After you, my lovely language!" (*OC* II, 276). Breton claims the absolute equality of every speaker and every writer confronted with "the automatic message" that dictates directly to them. When he emphasizes the Surrealist preference for verbal images over purely visual ones, he is of course speaking for the writers and not the painters, but the reason he gives for the preference is the greater *richness* of images verbally grasped. All the mannered effort of writers who have only talent falls short compared with the extraordinary profusion of images, sensations, and expression granted to the poet who is able to receive the dictated message in a "state of grace."[3] All the labored attempts at describing "Baudelairean correspondences" are already out of date, timid as they are in comparison to the "dream values" alone recognized by the Surrealists.[4] Pointing to other images in an endless sequence, Surrealist images are never frozen into a "perfect" poem or into any other rigid framework. A passage of the essay "Exposition X . . . , Y" calls anyone incapable of perceiving these images (such as a horse galloping on a tomato) an absolute cretin, calls the traditional poetic simile feeble, and, by its casual ending and absence of any effort to persuade, implies that the person who does not instantly accept this simple statement of all the multiple metamorphoses within the Surrealist vision is just as idiotic as the others.

A tomato is also a child's balloon,
Surrealism—I repeat—having suppressed
the word "like." The horse is about to
become one with the cloud, et cetera.

(*OC* II, 301)

In his "Introduction to the 'Contes Bizarres' d'Achim d'Arnim" Breton expands on the topic of the voluntary hallucination, of making oneself a seer in Rimbaud's sense, and of the extremely troubling effect such vision has on the notion of personality. As the exterior world undergoes, from our point of view, a change in appearance related to the more general "crisis of the object" that Breton finds characteristic of our time, as our doubt of accepted categories affects us in our turn, we are fated to undergo a crisis of personality. The contrary feelings of "double identity" and the loss of any personal certainty, in which "the notion of the *I* is shaken," exist side by side in the Surrealist believer. Not only must words be removed from their accustomed meanings and thus from their usual applications in a deliberate diversion from their ordinary meanings, but the poets themselves must be separated from all their accustomed settings and roots, be set loose in a state of utter bewilderment, *dépaysés,* and lost to their former being.

> Moreover, Surreality will be a function of our willingness to accept a complete "dépaysement" from everything (and it is understood that one can go as far as to "dépayser" a hand in isolating it from an arm, that this hand profits as a hand, and also that in speaking of "dépaysement," we are not only thinking of the possibility of acting in space. ("Notice to the reader of the 'Hundred Headed Woman'[5] of Max Ernst," *OC* II, 302ff.)

Others can go on clinging to family, country, and land—Breton and the Surrealists will take up the same slogans as in the time of DADA: leave everything . . . The Surrealist chooses isolation from others, with their herdlike values, in order to champion a permanent "dizzying exchange." Such pride helps to guarantee against complete breakdown. Breton himself, he says, has never worried about his own "interior equilibrium." Balancing the will to multiplicity and complexity is an equally strong will to unity; the latter has, needless to say, nothing whatsoever to do with the traditional notion of simplicity, since it continues to imply and include the multiple. In "Legitimate Defense," which begins with a eulogy of revolt as the agent of creativity, Breton describes at length the Surrealist's assurance of having been chosen—you might read it as "condemned"—to answer the call of the marvelous, which he calls a *summons:*

> It is an order which we have received once and for all and which we have never had an opportunity to dispute. It sometimes seems to us, and it is even rather paradoxical, that what we say is not what is most necessary to say and that there might be a better way of saying it. But it is as if we had been condemned to it for eternity. (*OC* II, 282)

The Surrealist writes from a metaphysical and moral need as compelling as any of the usual values accepted by non-Surrealists, and the act of writing effects a major unification of his personality against the exterior social ramifications of ordinary living. The mental state proper for receiving "the automatic message" is closely akin to the mental state of the primitive and the child, both of whom demonstrate a unique faculty, separated in the adult into the acts of perception and representation. The main role of automatism is to re-create the original identification of these two acts within the setting of a monistic, even "monotone" aesthetics and metaphysics, like that propagated by Count Keyserling, that proposes a unique being joining God, the Soul, and the world in one.

The vision from the state of Surrealist grace is often described as crystalline. Everything human is seen to be free from the diverse shadows of traditional categorizations, both individual and social, and of Western rationalism. At the end of his introduction to his "Discourse" essay, Breton invokes the "Orient of anger and of pearls" in an intense lyricism based stylistically on the play of dualities typical of Surrealism at its emotional peaks:

> You who are the shining image of my dispossession, Orient, beautiful bird of prey and of innocence, I implore you from the depth of the kingdom of shadows! Inspire me, so that I may be he who has no more shadow. (35)

It is natural that the greatest illumination should be visible in the works of artists, as they most frequently re-create the unique union of seeing and representing. The essay "Picasso in his Element" describes the lucid vision of the person freed from all ties rational, personal, and social, by a "desire for total consciousness" and an implacable realization of disintegration. For this person unafraid to confront as many different aspects in the world as in Picasso's paintings all possibilities are open; the world appears to be once more in a state of genesis that Breton calls "the great illumination," the crystalline chain "from which not one link is missing." In the paintings of Picasso runs the "marvelous, irresistible current" of luminous revelation in its harmony and force; we recognize the vocabulary of clarity: moments are "sparkling," by the place of the "radiant river."

Over this same "brilliant, inapproachable, magnetized river" Dali, like Picasso, refuses to lay down any bridges to reassure the average spectator. Here an unusual courage is required of all the Surrealists and participants in the Surrealist vision; they cannot retreat before anything that can in any way enlarge the field of imagination, and they must work for the reconstruction of Noah's Ark so that this time "it won't be the dove returning, but the crow." Fear threatens them at every step, in all the deserted landscapes of de Chirico, in all the odd re-creations of the artist's haunted fancy. Breton is convinced that unknown beings are lurking "in a sort of interior window, and they reverberate in *the air* as if the air were suddenly revealed to be a simple trick of glass panes which could be imperceptibly, but definitely, played with so that an immense hole could be made, where there would finally appear the beings— which we may or may not be able to exorcize—haunting a second land- scape that we cannot help but suspect" (88). Even these malicious "beings of prey" are to be sought out, since they are so far unknown. Just as the world of erotic imagination is valuable for its "kernel of night" so far not completely explored, so is any act or sensation not yet experienced to be tried.

Among these acts, that of automatic writing was, confesses Breton in "The Automatic Message" of 1933, valuable above all for its power to clear out the literary stable, to open the floodgates so that the old dull world of the already tried could be swept away, so that the adept could enter the new universe free and light from having abandoned the old baggage of logic, reason, and habit.

> The essential thing was that the *climate* of automatic productions made itself felt, that the mind got wind of a land whose flora and fauna were instantly recognizable, and especially whose *structure* (which was appar- ently the same for everyone) had only to be revealed. The hard part was to get people to try this recognition for themselves; to convince them that this land wasn't *elsewhere,* but in *themselves;* and to make them discard all their baggage so that their step would be light enough to cross the bridge leading there. (*C,* 65)

Desire and Motion

The ideal atmosphere, as Breton had said ten years before in the "Introduction to the Discourse . . . ," is one in which "what could exist destroys at every step what does exist." Nothing is inadmissible, there is no wish that cannot be carried out, even that of the frog who would like to be bigger than the ox. La Fontaine called such an animal foolish—not so the Surrealist: "It did not seem to me that any wish, even an animal one and of such a puerile kind, was incapable of perfect execution" (OC II, 279). The whole point of artistic creation is, as Breton says in the Picasso piece, to "affirm the hostility" that the creative being feels toward the exterior world and to "render the exterior object adequate to his desire, and thus to reconcile, to a certain extent, the being and the world" (OC II, 364). It is unquestionably valuable to express the "dialectical movement" of the mind. The finished work, however, is to be considered only an excretion in relation to the primary desire:

> Since it alone is truly suggestive of the power granted to man to act on the world to make it conform to himself (and in this way it is a fully revolutionary power), the uninterrupted temptation to confront all that exists with all that can exist, to bring forth from the never seen everything that can exhort the already seen to make itself less obvious seems far more precious to me. (OC II, 365)

Picasso's paintings convert the entire world to their own transparency and permit it to be reborn in an "interminable gestation" of *optimal* moments, for against the illusory power of the external world, the human will forms other beings as instants of intercession. Picasso never loses sight of the ephemeral nature of his creations, and it is in them that his work finds its particular radiance, all the brighter for declaring itself *temporary.*

The character of the Surrealist creation is constant motion; no Surrealist work proposes itself as eternal. If Breton envisages himself as a Theseus forever closed within a labyrinth of crystal, at least he intends to confer upon the labyrinth a movement as perpetual as his within it. Speaking of the poetry of René Char (in his "Letter to A. Rolland de Renéville"), Breton praises his crystalline union of transparency and hardness and takes for his definition of crystallization the Hegelian description of "the moment when the mobile and unresting activity of magnetism attains complete repose." He will echo, in other terms, this paradoxical union of movement and rest in his later definition of convulsive beauty, the beauty he thinks most appropriate to Surrealism. But here he means to stress not beauty but the inescapable and dynamic Hegelian dialectic of the mind:

> For my part I hold resolutely to this conception of thought which never ceases to oscillate between the consciousness of its perfect autonomy and that of its strict dependency . . . Consequently, for the future liberation of human thought, I count both on the sovereignty never yet realized within this thought alone and still always potentially contained there, and on the future of the exterior facts which is always susceptible to influence. (*OC* II, 331)

Breton's optimism is based on our ability to change our own language and thought processes, and with them, the world. The unknown is seen as a constant inspiration to action and to the mobility in which Breton places his ultimate faith.

Chapter Eight
1937: Mad Love

I would like my life to leave after it no other murmur than that of a watchman's song, of a song to while away the waiting. Independent of what happens and what does not happen, the wait itself is magnificent.

—*Mad Love*, 25

Conceiving Vision

The word "convulsive," which I use to describe the only beauty which should concern us, would lose any meaning in my eyes were it to be conceived in motion and not at the exact expiration of this motion. There can be no beauty at all, as far as I am concerned—convulsive beauty—except at the cost of affirming the reciprocal relations linking the object seen in its motion and in its repose. (*ML*, 10)

Breton's emphasis on *timing* here is crucial, and evident. The linking of love to death as to life marks the vital and mortal convulsions of the love, in its mad whirling about to quiet down. Such an emphasis is deeply baroque. More of a challenge still to the reading is the *conception* of the beauty: it is engendered, constructed, thought of, perceived *in relation*—as potentially absent, not there until it is *conceived*. This is heady stuff—not just body stuff, although it is that, too. The picture of the dancer turning rapidly makes its own comment on the sexuality of the thing—nevertheless, *conception does it*. The vision makes the emotion happen.

Unique Loving

The change of emphasis from *Communicating Vessels* to *Mad Love* is unmistakable, from the will to collective revolutionary action to the acceptance of the *"lyric behavior"* or the poetic style of a smaller group. There are nuances to this change; for instance, even in *Communicating Vessels* the actual split between the Surrealist idea of revolution and that usually attributed to the Communist party is evident, as is the split between Breton as an individual and the many he observes. And even in *Mad Love,* Breton continues to claim that the rule of capitalism complicates the difficulties of unique love. He observes in *Mad Love* that the earlier work was limited by his not having wanted to cut himself off from "practical action" at that time; because, he says, the passage from words to actions was in fact not permitted to him, he finds himself free to re-examine the questions of dream, of chance, and of desire.

We have seen before and shall see again what is required by this now fully accepted lyrical or Surrealist behavior—Breton specifically equates the two. It is the principal rule of Surrealist vision, the always renewing faith in the always renewed. It is, broadly restated, that the known should not be overestimated in relation to the unknown.

So all the ways of *new knowing* are to be treasured. Dreams, for instance. The dream cannot be completely analyzed at a time contemporary with it, because it must, like poetry, remain open to the future. The prime example is Breton's own "Sunflower" poem of 1923, quoted in entirety in *Mad Love* at the moment the narrator, Breton, meets a "young woman," Jacqueline Lamba. The conception of beauty, then, takes place eleven years after the original conception of the poem, as if, indeed, the senseless motion of "pre-conception" were to settle down into a presumably lasting conception. On that May night when he meets Jacqueline and walks with her in the "Night of the Sunflower," it all works. It proves, too, that poems cannot be fully satisfying in their properly predictive role until their full significance is seen developing its own justification, which was once invisible to the poet as well as the reader.

Now it is time for Breton the man to regret the changes Breton the poet made to this poem to render it more "pleasing" and less obscure. The regret is certainly justified, even from the purely "aesthetic" point of view from which Surrealist work is not supposed to be judged— although, ironically, Breton's own work is unquestionably "satisfactory" by the most exigent and enlightened aesthetic standards. Once its predictive elements had been realized, the corrections instantly appear, in retrospect, as *faults* of vision. Aesthetic considerations can ruin the most convincing convulsion, especially with a time lapse. The time lapse makes the corrections look like judgment lapses.

Fragments from the poem keep occurring to him, as if they were "tapping" on the window of his consciousness in the same way that the sentences of his half-waking state had done, described in the *First Manifesto.*

Those quotations, I must admit, were still tapping on that window, but quite faintly, and I had, on that same afternoon, to go out and wander around alone before I noticed that a remarkable need for cohesion had taken hold of them, that they would not let me go until they had been returned to the entity, organic or not, to which they belonged. So I was led, only in the evening, to reopen one of my books at the page where I knew I would pick them out. This concession to everything I hadn't wanted to know until then turned out to be a brilliant and uninterrupted suite of discoveries. (ML, 55)

Discoveries: they work forward and backward, discovering in and for the moment, and then after. This story is a story of the Surrealist marvelous . . . Surrealism sees the world as a forest of analogical indications, but it considers them far more dynamic and more revolutionary in their implications than the Baudelairean correspondences, as has already been suggested. The *insolite,* or the necessarily unusual appearance of things indispensable to Surrealist vision, is not easily accepted (even by Breton), nor is the fact that the exterior world seems to arrange itself for the benefit of the unconscious desire of the individual, whose responsibility is to always remain open to the workings of chance. The Surrealist leap of faith is in every case accompanied by an inner doubt as essential to its particular character as the distance between the two poles of the Surrealist image is to the force of that image. "I confess I am hesitant to take this leap, fearing a fall into some endless unknown. Shadows of all sorts swirl rapidly about me, creating high walls whose lack of substance I am powerless to prove" (ML, 39).

The *"insolite"* and the *"faits-précipices"* that embody it are a definite cause of fear, and, at the same time, the clearest example of the marvelous junctions that Breton makes the centers of his books, the "necessary" communications between human beings and things, the mental and the material, the subjective and the objective, in short, the frequent manifestations near to us of the *sublime point,* which is never quite within our reach. Most of the Surrealist games are directed at creating the greatest possible number of these junctions—for example, the game of definitions, where the participants have no idea what object they are defining. Re-creations of language, revision of the standard purpose of things, multiplication of images—which are only instruments capable of forcing the universe to give up its opacity for an only partially obscured clarity—are the goals of Surrealist play.

Both in the place they occupy and the importance Breton attaches to them, the two central images of this book are privileged. The locomotive stopped at its greatest speed in a virgin forest represents the perfect junction of mobility and immobility—Breton calls it a monument "to victory and to disaster." An example of convulsive beauty (whose sexual implications are clear), it represents an ideal and permanent state of what is in ordinary life a transient rapidity of movement, as well as its destruction "in the exact moment of its expiration." The image that is its counterpart in the constantly balanced structure of Surrealism is the far more famous one of the crystal, also implying the perfection of motion stilled (here Breton refers to Hegel). Concentrated into a smaller space than the first image and therefore carrying an even greater potential force, the crystal is the guiding image of many Surrealist works. A combination of complexity (in its facets) and simplicity of form, of the clarity and the spontaneous hardness both Dada and Surrealism oppose to the laborious *work* and the weak sentimentality of bourgeois taste and morality, the crystal is the ultimate Surrealist aspiration: "the key to the fields lies in the crystal."[1]

"Love with its retinue of clarities," "this chain of illuminations passing through us," love "as an apparatus of mirrors," "enabling us to create a diamond from the blackest of nights":[2] of all the perfect condensations and marvelous junctions, human love is the most crystalline for Breton. By its nature it refuses any separation between the human and the natural worlds, so Breton can identify the woman he loves with "the snow of mountain peaks at sunrise." The miraculous embodiment of dizziness (*"le vertige"*) joined with the odd mobile/immobile permanence of convulsive spontaneous beauty, irrational Surrealist love is mad in its complete freedom from the limits of logic and from the nuances and vicissitudes of intellect. But, inescapably, the theme of human judgment enters. *Mad Love,* which ends with Breton's hope that his little daughter be "madly loved" and which takes as its motif the positive value of such love, begins with a disquisition on variations, on the procession of beings loved and of the "selves" that loved them, as if, seen in the most trivial light, this sort of preface indicates a conscience not at rest with itself (or, in fact, the sense of malediction of which Breton speaks here). That the last chapter should have been written when Jacqueline had left him was enough to place it under a cloud; the reader who did not know this[3] could have detected, in any case, the solemnity of warning. Marguerite Bonnet ascribes the proliferation of fairy tale décors in the book itself (especially in the fifth part) to part of a willed escape into fantasy from a love that was itself difficult and, at the same time, to indications of menace in the center of a loving plenitude: a dragon, snakes, vines, a fatal flower, and Bluebeard himself.[4]

Of course, many writers and readers would choose to have loved only one being. And yet, in the beginning of *Mad Love,* all the successive figures Breton imagines seated on two facing benches and judging him represent unique moments of sincere conviction. He has been all those past images of himself and he has loved all those corresponding images; the synthesis he longs for is attainable only if all the past beings were prefigurations of the present one, who is in all senses ultimate. Parallel to this solution of synthesis is one of multiplication. As the various are one, so the one is various:

> Because you are unique, you can't help being for me always another, another you. Across the diversity of these inconceivable flowers over there, it is you over there changing whom I love in a red blouse, naked, in a gray blouse. (*ML,* 81)

This repetition, which he likens to that of one single plant growing always taller, is, like the crystal, like the art of the insane, and like the word "always," a "key to the limitless fields."

But at the moment of grace, just when the synthesis is to be realized, Breton undergoes a mental crisis of confidence in himself, parallel to the doubt he felt before at exposing himself to the indispensable perils of the *insolite:*

> What am I capable of after all, and what shall I do so as not to be unworthy of such a fate? I walk ahead automatically, in a great clank of gates being closed. To love, to find once more the lost grace of the first moment when one is in love. . . . All sorts of defenses take shape around me, bright laughter springing up from the years past to finish sobbing, under the great beating of gray wings of an uncertain spring night. . . . Who goes with me at this hour in Paris without leading me and whom, moreover, I am not leading? I never remember having felt in my life such a great weakness. I almost lost sight of myself. (*ML,* 44)

And, accompanied by the woman desperately loved in what should be a profoundly marvelous and, above all, genuine moment, Breton feels the moment threatened by the same sense of the artificial that had eventually ruined Nadja's words for him: "The conversation . . . now grazes only the mask of things. I fear I am letting it slip into the artificial in spite of myself" (*ML,* 45). Only in stories does doubt never creep in. Here his heightened sensitivity only aggravates the pessimism of his vision, and, in a state of uncertainty corresponding to the cloudy spring night, he echoes once more his questioning at the beginning of *Nadja* (*"Who am I?"*):

> I see bad and good in all their native state, the bad winning out with all the ease of suffering. . . . Life is slow, and man scarcely knows how to play it. . . . Who is going with me, who is preceding me tonight once again? . . . There would still be time to turn back. (*ML,* 45)

But all the uncertainty and suffering does finally contribute to the Surrealist idea of mad love at its maddest. As Breton explains to his daughter at the end, the night of the "Sunflower" would have been far less radiant without the preceding misery, as the notion of the crystal, in Surrealism, always includes obscurity. That may perhaps seem a facile, or at least an obvious, resolution of the difficulty.

More interesting is that this moment of hesitation and even anguish while Breton and his future wife are walking around Paris is exactly paralleled by another such moment while the two of them are walking down a Brittany shore, near Lorient. During the latter, a serious *irrational* irritation overcomes Breton, and although he later explains it by the proximity of a malevolent object (in this case a particular house, the "Blocked Fort," which is in turn parallel to an "evil mask" previously mentioned), the "explanation" does not change the fact that the moment exists as a *hole* in the "chain of illumination," which it has interrupted. It is not too strong to say that Breton is obsessed with *discontinuity,* of which all the images of arrested motion are only the positive side, and that they are balanced by others, more threatening: "And in addition, the real problem, so far as I saw it, had always been something else: Is the mirror of love between two beings likely to be clouded over by the very fact of circumstances totally foreign to love and to be unclouded, suddenly, when these circumstances cease? Yes" (*ML,* 110). So, "The mirror clouds over. . . ."

Breton proclaims, in describing the *sublime point* at the close of the book, that he has only wanted to know the triumphal hours of love, and maintains that his own occasional incapacity or lack of faith subtracts nothing from the great hope he places in "mad love." That he could write this is testimony to his faith in writing itself, for this is the story of *Mad Love,* which can be told now. The first five parts are written (two, far earlier), and he is working at top speed, Breton writes to Jacqueline in early September of 1936, to finish the sixth part, the story of their walk. Suddenly, on September 6, there is a blow-up, and Jacqueline leaves Breton with their tiny daughter, and goes to Ajaccio. When he finishes the last part of *Mad Love,* the letter to "Chipnut of Munkhazel," he does not know if she will return. The grave tone of the letter, its wish for his daughter to be *madly loved,* rings all the more solemnly.

Surrealist love, since it is still a human love, includes the moments of necessary despair inflicted by the universe, but is in no way defeated by them: "I do not deny that love has a difference with life. I say it should vanquish, and in order to do so, should rise to such a poetic conscious- ness of itself that every hostile thing it meets should melt in the hearth of its own splendor" (*ML,* 116). To his faith in the continuous and the multiple—the faith that the woman loved includes not only all the past women loved, but is herself many women—this fear of the discontinu- ous is an echo. Seen in another light, it seems a complementary faith: the hope of Surrealism itself lies in the definitive novelty of each new moment. "Tomorrow will be another, completely torn off from yester- day." Befitting the drama of Surrealism, this is in no way a tranquil faith, but a violent one: "torn off" (*"déchiré"*). The resolution of these faiths takes place in Surrealist love as it is expressed in one of the most famous of all Surrealist lines: "Always for the first time."

The convulsive beauty mentioned at the end of *Nadja* and perfectly corresponding in a positive sense to the opening uncertainty takes on an additional complexity here, almost ten years later. The permanence of discontinuity, like the arresting of violent motion at the moment of its expiration, creates an exceptional intensity within each moment, an intensity so great that, against all the rational warnings of the outside world, it does not permit the prediction of any decadence, or any degra- dation in time. Regardless of all *variations,* when Breton speaks of the battle between the notions of "forever" and "for a long time," he shows no hesitation:

> Of these two expressions, the one that wears my colors, even if its star may be waning now, even if it must lose, is *forever.* . . . What I have loved, whether I have kept it or not, I shall love *forever.* (*ML,* 114)

The irrationality of Surrealist love will save it from the cautions of reason. Nadja, in her extreme of irrationality, was not saved, yet who is to say that her aloneness did not always haunt Breton, not only in his moments of doubt ("Who goes with me?"), but also in his moments of

faith? For a certain loneliness pierces through the optimism even when
Breton is defining love as a union of two beings in a prelogical state of
grace, and it can be interpreted, like his self-questioning, as an echo of
her own:

> There would still be time to turn back. (*ML,* 45) . . . the fusion restores
> to all things the lost colors of the time of ancient suns, where, however,
> solitude also rages . . . (10)

Chapter Nine

Poetry: *"Lieu de reconciliation"*

Reading a Surrealist Poem

Surrealism is based on contrast of will and perception: the will to *link* and the constant perception of *contraries*. Tension between these two elements at the source furnishes the initial energy and ongoing dynamism of Surrealist poetry.

This tension is sensed in the individual verses—first, in the necessary distance between the two elements of the image, since the Surrealists accept Reverdy's celebrated dictum that it is always the polarity of these elements that creates the momentum for the shock of the image, and second, because each image is itself put into a succession of images, sustaining the energy and building on the dynamism. Although at first glance the images may seem to build a series of descriptions less shocking than successive and cumulative, unless the overall impression is as much one of contrary perceptions as of linking, the poem is probably not successful as a Surrealist work. Even though the tensions of a Surrealist poem cannot always be described (that is, one cannot always say: this represents a tension between A and B), the sensitive reader must be in some fashion aware of it.

Surrealism is less an individual attitude than that of a group. In similar fashion, a Surrealist poem is often seen with a greater range of nuances in its relations with other Surrealist poems than alone. As happens with the radically contrasting elements of the image, when Surrealist poems are juxtaposed they are each cast in a new light—harsh, peculiar, intensifying.

Consider the images of three poems from *L'Air de l'eau*, a collection of fourteen (an echo of the fourteenth of August, the day of his marriage to Jacqueline Lamba) untitled poems. The poems are linked in a watery sequence, from which I have chosen those beginning "L'aigle sexuel exulte," "Il allait être cinq heures," and "Ils vont tes membres."

In all three, the predominating images are of wings (of an eagle, of the woman loved), of clarity (clear days, a glass newspaper, a mirror, an electric light, sunbeams, windowpanes and glaziers, water, a prismatic bed), of Breton's favorite color, green (mint, emerald, foliage and particular leaves, green sheets and green eyebrows like those of Jacqueline Lamba at this time, a willow), and of a sense of danger (an incision, scars, the loss of leaves and the ripping of the veins from a leaf, a leaf slippery and with no edges, saws, a dagger, blood). Jacqueline was living on the Faubourg Saint-Jacques near a maternity hospital at this time; thus the mingling of sexuality and hope of a birth and peril.

The links between one image and another can be seen as both evident and implied on the levels of vision, imagination, and wordplay: from the bright and liquid air in the first poem to the liquid wing in the third, from windowpanes in the first and second poems to the glaziers in the third; from the sexual image at the opening of the first poem to the bifurcation and the mingling of the blood in the second to the three references to the bed in the third; from the *"manches"* (sleeves) in the first poem to the *"manche"* (handle) of the dagger in the second and from the *"verre"* (glass) to the *"ver luisant"* (glowworm) in the second poem to the *"draps verts"* (green sheets) in the third. The contrasts and tensions seem inseparable from the linking. In the first poem a descending and an ascending wing are joined in two successive lines, and death and life of birth and rebirth are joined in the same line; similarly the images of cold (snow, icebergs, and frozen particles in the first, icicles in the second) contrast with the sexual images. In the second poem, falling and rising are opposed a few lines apart, while joy is apparent in the exhalation of grief, and the rustling of flowers and the icicles meet in the same line. Furthermore there is an implied and important opposition of the hermetic to the crystal-clear.[1] Paradigmatic of the linking process—which makes its own opposition to the oppositions already mentioned—the coral handle of the dagger which bifurcates does so in order to join the blood of the lovers with that coral, of its same color. The repetitions of certain words within the poems serve as simple carriers for the meeting of imagery thus reinforced: *"son aile . . . son aile," "au premier rayon, dans ce rayon," "un cri, un cri."* Finally, in the last poem, the bell towers join.

Furthermore, the overall "theme" of *L'Air de l'eau* as of each of its poems individually is clearly one of linking, as in the title, the air of water): the linking of love in the sexual union of opposites, the conceptual union between love and life, and the linguistic union between the clear air and the clear wing, all *in spite of* the more ominous linking of life with danger and death. The rise and fall of the eagle's wings, the falling star, and the diving bell rising all reflect the positive rhythm of lovemaking as

surely as they do the tragic uncertainty of human fortunes: the dangerous and yet exalted image of the dagger's bifurcation is the central one
here. The freshness of clarity and of green indicates birth and rebirth, as
do the allusions to the maternity hospital and, in the first poem, to the
oneiric potential in each person loved and in the imagination of the
poet:

> Alors des étendues jettent l'ancre se déploient au fond de mon oeil fermé
>
> (Then great expanses cast their anchor and range themselves in the depths
> of my closed eye)

As Breton's red pepper becomes a dragonfly in the mode recommended by the oriental sage Bashô, the poem goes positive. When the
"green sheets," which might after all have been associated with mold, are
joined to the cycle of rebirth and later compared to an almond, the
whole bed takes on a marvelous prismatic transparency. Within the
world of Surrealist poetry, all things are probably true, and the only
betrayal is to *limit their force.*

Each of the poems ends with union. The first unites the poet and the
world; the second, the poet and the woman loved: the third, where the
bed/sailboat is a liquid wing beating in the song of the window makers
(or, by extension, in the poetry of the Surrealist), is a union of love and
adventure, an exultation in transformations and in clarity. Together, the
poems reinforce each other in their contrasts and their tensions, in their
associations and their conclusions—as should always be the case with
poems from the same collection. On a larger scale, all the most genuine
Surrealist poems can be considered as belonging to the same collection.
Most of Breton's best poems, and those of the other Surrealists, show the
"Free Union" he extols between the poet and the woman, between the
poem and the universe it mirrors, between the poet's perception and his
representation: This union is the convergence of all his work, of the hermetic and the clear.

"Puis la poésie aux phares rouges sur une mer toute brune"

Breton's poems should not be discussed in isolation from one another; unlike ordinary "texts," they are witnesses to the poetic spirit rather
than examples of individual creation. Nor should they be separated

from discussions of his "theories" as purely lyric statements. Surrealism is, or wills itself to be, a unifying force, and such "lyricism" as there is cannot be dissociated from Surrealist beliefs: they are linked with the *fil conducteur* or conducting wire that runs through all Surrealist discourse, thought, and practice as ultimate link. In Surrealism, nothing is superfluous, and within the realm of Surrealist concern, all is of equal importance.

The long and important *Ode à Charles Fourier* serves as an example of the joining of theory and poetry. In this one poem it is an easy matter to find references, however glancing, to almost all of the main Surrealist attitudes. Here Breton rails against the "stupid anesthesia of flags," implying in that expression all the assembled menaces of nations, families, wars, religions, all of which dull the instinct for anything new and the unexplored. Here he attacks, with Fourier, all the "immobilistic" thinkers who would prevent the constant *motion* to which the Surrealists are committed; he insists on the value of the world of sleep but refuses at the same time to acknowledge the single utility of any one *lever* on the machine, that is, of any one process or theory. He insists on the ritual and the optimistic aspect of the *"sens de la fête"* (the latter word including the several religious and secular meanings of feast, celebration, festival) and on the necessity of maintaining "the integrity of the word," with all its religious connotations as well its literary-verbal ones. But here too Breton laments the necessary brevity of the *"images fugaces,"* their essentially fleeting quality. The catalog of theories directly referred to or indirectly implied could be extended and a similar one drawn up for the other long poems such as *Les Etats-Généraux* and *Fata Morgana.*

In all of these, the interpenetration of theory and poetic text is visible.

"L'alphabet secret de la toute-nécessité" (1940)

The connection between the alchemy of the word and Surrealist work is intimate and constant. For the Surrealist, the word itself is eternally fascinating:

Le ventre des mots est doré ce soir et rien n'est plus en vain
(The body of words is gilded tonight and nothing is any longer in vain—
"Ligne Brisée")

Expression *is* thought—it is not an adjunct, or a transcription, or in any way to be considered subsequent to thinking. It is in some cases, as in automatic writing, prior to thought. And in others, thought's contemporary language is incantation: the mention at the close of "Hôtel des étincelles" of a book inscribed with the words *No tomorrow* lends a retrospective horror to the entire poem, a horror prepared by the image of a "hellish window" in the third line. The sentiment seems to depend as much on the literal sight of the words as on their actual content. *Fata Morgana* describes furniture heavier empty than were it to be filled with sand; Breton calls for word-levers to remove it. The uttering of the word is sufficient, as simple imagining of the imagination is not. Always, even after the initial enthusiasm of automatic writing had passed, Breton claimed that the vision came *after* the words that stated it. He never ceased to insist on the perpetual possibility of *any* miracle solicited by speech:

> Et pour une fois ne se peut-il que l'expression *pour la vie* déclenche une des aurores boréales dont sera fait le tapis de table du Jugement Dernier?
>
> (And for once may not just the expression *for life* be enough to produce an aurora borealis like those of which the tablecloth of the Last Judgment will be made?) (38)

The preceding example, which fuses the present, the future, and the eternal, is taken from the collection *Clair de terre,* its title another fusion of terms and of vision (*"clair de lune"* = moonlight, so *"clair de terre"* = earthlight, to emphasize the quotidian nature of the marvelous). Such fusions are responsible both for "L'Air de l'eau" and for the last line of a poem about a wild flame (*"flamme barbare"*): "Flamme d'eau guide-moi jusqu'à la mer de feu (Flame of water lead me to the sea of fire)." Surrealist language, for which the Surrealist image is a model, is frequently a joining or "telescoping" of partial or complete elements to make untried compounds. From what is not yet known comes the precipitate of the marvelous.

Such a concentration of language and thought is doubled by an opposite process of expansion: the mention of a term provokes the mention of another in some way like it, and then a series of images appropriate to both, in deliberate branchings of ambiguity out from the original simple vision or expression. This process is so rapid as to leave no lingering preciosity, only a series of what seem to be "marvelous" coincidences. Thus a ruby leads to a rose, which will lead to the similar sound of dew (*"rosée"*), and any of these may suggest to a fish called *"rouget"* ("Au beau demi-jour," *L'Air*) as easily as the color rose leads visually to the color red (*"rouge"*), or the sound "rose" to a rose window (*"rosace"* in "Hôtel des étincelles," *Le Revolver*). A fistful of anything, which is similar to a handle by association of meaning as well as sound (both are *"poignée"*), leads to the sword that one grips (*"poignard"*) by simple repetition (*"Il allait être cinq heures,"* *L'Air*)—although the resulting poem is often a complicated jigsaw puzzle in which the simplicity is apparently lost. The quantities of puns (*"la mourre, l'amour,"* Les Etats-Généraux, *"le coeur m'en dit, le coeur mendie,"* "Toutes les écolierès ensemble," *Le Revolver*) and interior echoes such as those in Breton's famous poem for Jacqueline Lamba, significantly entitled *L'Union libre* (*"aux mollets de modelle"* *"au cou d'orge . . . à la gorge . . . d'or"*), develop a verbal richness that would be cloying, were it not so brief. Nothing dwells long in Surrealism, whose moods are always shifting:

> Au dos de lumière
> à la nuque de pierre roulée et de craie mouillée
> Et de chute d'un verre dans lequel on vient de boire
> (Her back of light
> Her nape of crushed stone and moistened chalk
> And the fall of a glass from which one has
> just finished drinking)

A sense of danger is retained throughout the poem, enhancing both the oppositions and the visuality:

> Ma femme aux seins de creuset du rubis
> Aux seins de spectre de la rose sous la rosée
> (My wife with breasts of the crucible of ruby
> With breasts of the spectre of the rose under
> the dew)

The color extends from the fire implied in the crucible to the rose lost (and haunting) under the dewdrops as the syllable "rose" haunts the word *"rosée."* Breton uses, perhaps unconsciously—which in no way invalidates or changes the tenor of that use—a whole range of references of this nature. The range stretches from a simple association and transfer, in which the middle term is present by implication—so the "lacerat-

ed curtains" lead to the "book scribbled in," through the ambiguity of
the middle term *"griffé"* = scratched, like lacerated, and also scribbled
("Hôtel des étincelles," *Le Revolver*). Again, the chopping of a tree leads
to the "cordes" of a musical instrument, through the middle term "cord
of wood," a term that is absent but implied ("Les Attitudes spectrales,"
Le Revolver). In more complicated examples, the middle or *mediator,* term
may be suppressed altogether:

> La crêpe qu'il faut lancer si haut pour la dorer . . .
>
> La crêpe magique le sceau aérien . . .
>
> (The crêpe you have to flip so high to make it golden . . .
>
> The magic crêpe the airy seal . . .) (81)

Here the word *"sceau"* is a homonym for the absent term *saut* (leap),
associated with the tossing or jump of the pancake into the air ("J'ai
devant moi," *L'Air*).

The intricate and beautiful prose poem on despair called "Le Verbe
être" reveals a great range of mood/sound/concept contrasts:

> Je me lève chaque jour comme tout le monde et je détends les bras sur un
> papier à fleurs, je ne me souviens de rien et c'est toujours avec désespoir
> que je découvre les beaux arbres déracinés de la nuit. . . . Il fait un temps
> de temps.
>
>   (I get up every day like everyone else and I stretch out my arms on a
> floral wallpaper, I remember nothing and it is always with despair that I
> discover the beautiful uprooted trees of the night. . . . It is a weather of
> time.) (86)

The implied natural optimism of a normal, shared quotidian arising
in the day contrasts with despair and the nocturnal storm, as does the
artificial calm of the wallpaper, although the paper flowers are in their
imitation of the real as uprooted from their "natural" surroundings as are
the storm-wracked trees. The final mockery of our ordinary language
echoes the despair and negativity of forgetting everything and the sameness of "every day" and "everyone else," since even a weather fit for dogs
(*"temps de chien"*) or any such expression would have been less hollow than
this weather, which only repeats itself (literally, "time of time" or "weather of weather") as if the doubled, mirrored words were also "uprooted"
from their sense, any sense. The passage spins in emptiness like an
empty life.

Of course no wordplay or image play would be particularly significant were it not for Breton's absolute conviction that rearrangements or re-creations of language and conception and vision touch not just language, conception, and vision, but the universe beyond them. His stubborn refusal to *separate* or distinguish realms of activity confers on all those realms an equal importance or nonimportance. Inevitably, the mode of expression of one poem or all of Breton's poems is no less serious than his ideas themselves. His texts often ambiguously turn toward the positive or the negative depending on how they are read, challenging the reading and the world.

"Le cristal noir"

The apposition of diametrically opposed elements forms the basis for much Surrealist writing and for the "shock" of its style, whether it be spontaneous or deliberate. The contrasting images, if not in themselves of an extreme intricacy, compose the basic and even simple structure that holds together the complexities of vision.

Although some of the contrasts are conceptual (saved and lost, good and bad), some are slightly more complicated, combining the visual with the conceptual like the ascending and descending wings; for example, "le coup de revolver le sang qui saute lestement les marches vertes" ("the shot the blood skipping nimbly over the green steps"), where the implicit wounding contrasts with the briskness of the motion and the red color with the green of the steps, the latter implying freshness, spring, and rebirth, while the former implies life and vitality as well as suffering, in an ambiguity of content as well as of vision. To take another example, in Breton's identification[2] of the woman with "[u]ne haute flamme couchée dans la neige (a high flame lying in the snow)," the red of the flame contrasts directly with the white of the snow, as well as the heat with the cold, and the flame's relative height with the horizontal position of woman and flame (as opposed to simply contrasts of heat and cold like "le rayon se posa sur la fenêtre gelée/the sunbeam came to rest on the frozen window"; 201).

But the great majority of Breton's images by far are oppositions of light and dark, clarity and shadow. Such oppositions reappear constantly in the poetry associated with Surrealism, and especially in that of Tristan Tzara, Louis Aragon, and Paul Eluard; for any of these poets, one can make an almost endless catalogue of light/dark alternations, sometimes identified with rapid changes of mood but sometimes a mere spectacle.

Of course, much politically involved writing is of this sort, where the
good and the bad are clearly identifiable; these are the political
Surrealists, who leave Surrealism for a radical form of ideological commitment. In the following examples from Breton's poetry, typical and to
which many more could have been added, the obvious light/dark oppositions are italicized:

> le soleil *blanc* et *noir*
>
> (the white and black sun) (71)
>
> ses lances *blanches* et *noires*
>
> (its white and black lances (227)
>
> Une voiture *noire* rapide
>
> Couronnée d'aigles de *nacre*
>
> (A fast black car
>
> Crowned with mother-of-pearl eagles) (160–61)
>
> Page de *brune* au béret de cendre *blanche* . . .
>
> (Page of dusk with a beret of white ashes, "Le Volubilis et je sais
>
> l'hypotenuse")
>
> Ici le temps *se brouille* à la fois et *s'éclaire*
>
> (Here the weather clouds over and grows clear at the same time) (189)
>
> On dirait qu'on bat des cartes de *miroir* dans *l'ombre*
>
> (You would think they were shuffling mirror cards in the shadow) (215)
>
> Jersey Guernsey par temps *sombre* et *illustre*
>
> (Jersey Guernsey in dark and shining weather) (218)
>
> Est-ce l'amour ces doigts qui pressent la cosse du *brouillard*
>
> Pour qu'en jaillissent les villes inconnues aux portes hélas *éblouissantes*
>
> L'amour ces fils télégraphiques qui font de la *lumière insatiable* un *bril-*
>
> *liant* sans cesse qui se rouvre
>
> De la taille même de notre compartiment de *la nuit*
>
> Tu viens à moi de plus loin que *l'ombre* . . .
>
> (Is it love these fingers pressing on the husk of the fog
>
> To make the unknown towns with alas dazzling doors spring forth
>
> Love these telegraphic wires that make of insatiable light a ceaseless dia-
>
> mond reopening

As large as our compartment of night

You come to me from farther off than shadow . . .) (186)

Sometimes a whole poem is entirely constructed around the alternation from light to dark, as is "Le Sphinx vertébral," which opens with the shadow curved and patiently hovering about the paving stones and, after a few lines, switches to the scene of *"ce matin, proue du Soleil"* ("this morning prow of the Sun"), where the sense of adventure and movement contrasts with the slower-moving shadow. Now glaciers melt in a ray of light, and a wolf with glass (crystal) teeth is described growling at twilight amid the "smoking little fires" lighting up the turnips. White birds appear, darkening a casement window by their flight and laying black eggs. Finally, the poem moves in time from the simple juxtaposition of contraries:

Il fait jour à gauche mais complètement nuit à droite

(It is day on the left side but completely black on the right side)

to the progress from one toward another seen in the conclusion of the poem as the slow working of a primitive machine:

Les guetteuses se penchent se penchent[3] aux fenêtres

De tout leur côté d'ombre de tout leur côté de lumière

La bobine du jour est tirée par petits coups du côté du paradis de sable

Les pédales de la nuit bougent sans interruption

(The watchers lean, lean at their windows

From their whole side of shadow from their whole side of light

Bit by bit the bobbin of the day is pulled toward the side of the paradise of sand

The pedals of the night move without stopping) (102)

"Eclats de midi" ("bursts of noon"), *"Verres de lampes"* ("panes of the lamp"), *"Polis mes yeux"* ("my eyes polished" or "polish my eyes"), *"O vitres superposés de la pensée/Dans la terre de verre"*[4] (Oh layered windowpanes of thought/In the glass earth): the ideal of Surrealism is undoubtedly one of radiance and illumination, of the crystal and the marvelous. Yet it is not so simple as it might appear at first, of which the very proliferation of

the contraries is an indication. In this context, the alchemical lesson is invaluable, for it is within the dark that the light is to be found. Tzara declares in a *Note sur la poésie:* "Obscurity is productive if it is a light so white and pure that our neighbors are blinded by it,"[5] and Breton frequently associates sparks, mirrors, and even diamonds with shadow, dust, and fog—*"Glace de ténèbres miroir d'amour"* ("Looking-glass of shadow mirror of love," 148); *"l'éclatante poussière"* ("the radiant dust," 214).

In a similar fashion, the transferences, fusions, and reversals effected during the alchemical work are characteristic also of Surrealist vision. The preferred Surrealist game is that of *"l'un dans l'autre"* (one within the other), where the players accustom themselves to the *derivation* of objects from other objects in some way like them, the best example being the match, which contains the lion in potentiality because of the resemblance of the match flame to the mane of the lion. Thus in Breton's poems, we see the forest (the woods or like the wood handle) *within* the hatchet, or, in another sort of transference, the bars on the inside of the cage. These *inversions* of vision are typically Surrealist, and they are, like the alternations and ambiguities of form, responsible in large part for the supposed hermeticism of much Surrealist work. It is difficult in the sense that alchemical work is meant to be difficult: the uninitiated will stumble. But for the others—and only to the extent that a non-Surrealist is not doomed to be an eternal noninitiate—at least a partial illumination is possible.

"Et mouvement encore"

In his "qualité de convulsionnaire," the Surrealist has an innate tendency toward adventure and danger. As convulsive beauty depends on the shock of contrast, on the deliberate and yet spontaneous tensions created, for instance, between great momentum and absolute paralysis, high speed and total rest, the sense of adventure depends at least partly on the danger/pleasure contrast. Inferior in number only to the contrasts of light and dark are those of luxury and suffering, voluptuousness and violence, similar to those found in the Gothic novel, to which the Surrealists are so attached:

> Le vrai luxe
> C'est que le divan capitonné de satin blanc
> Porte l'étoile de la lacération
> (Real luxury

Is for the divan covered in white satin
To carry the star of laceration) (173)
D'un coup de baguette ç'avaient été les fleurs
Et le sang
(At a wave of the stick it was flowers
And blood) (201)

There is no better example of this juxtaposition/identification than in
the poem entitled "Les Ecrits s'en vont." Beginning with a voluptuous
image (found also in Tristan Tzara's *L'Homme approximatif* of 1930):

Des bras qui ne s'articulent à rien d'autre qu'au danger exceptionnel
d'un corps fait pour l'amour
Dont le ventre appelle les soupirs détachés des buissons pleins de voiles
Et qui n'a de terrestre que l'immense vérité glacée des traineaux de
regards sur l'étendue toute blanche
De ce que je ne reverrai plus
A cause d'un bandeau⁶ merveilleux
Qui est le mien dans le colin-maillard des blessures
(Arms connected only to the exceptional danger of the body made for
love
Whose belly summons sighs detached from thickets full of veils
And who has nothing earthly but the immense frozen truth of the
sleighs of looks on the all-white space
Of that which I shall not see again
Because of a marvelous band
Which is mine in the blindman's buff of wounds) (88)

Because of the interconnections of the Surrealist spirit, the distance
experienced between the opposite poles of the image or the opposite
moods of the poem (which are joined in an insufferable/marvelous com-
pound) is a distance easily translated in terms of a voyage, just as the distance between Rimbaud's *Je* and *autre* can be said, poetically, to inspire
(or even to produce) not only the *Illuminations* but also the journey of the
"Bateau ivre." At least four of the poems in the collection *Le Revolver à
cheveux blancs* alone are centered on images of motion and journeys.

The first, "La Mort rose," actually begins as an echo of "Le Bateau ivre":

> Les pieuvres ailées guideront une dernière fois la barque
> (The winged devil-fish will guide the boat one last time)

It then moves on to active descriptions (of the horizon opening, of a girl dancing, of the poet climbing, then walking at a rapid pace), and of a final loneliness characteristic of the Surrealist alternation between hope and despair.

A far more interesting poem, more complex and more explicitly involved with the literary adventure, is "Dernière levée," the "subject" of which is a letter whose stamp is obliterated by the zodiac and on which Breton's name is almost indecipherable. The atmosphere of uncertainty and menace continues:

> Quand elle me parviendra le soleil sera froid
> Il y aura des épaves sur la place Blanche
> Parmi lesquelles se distinguera mon courage
>
> (When it reaches me the sun will be cold
> There will be shipwrecks on the Place Blanche
> Among which my courage will stand out)

He opens the letter immediately, *"d'un coup de rame"* (literally, with an oar stroke, the expression *d'un coup*—at once—leading to the singularly appropriate image of the oar), and then his own voyage in the ship, formed of words never yet heard—and therefore marvelous—will correspond to the one the letter has made to reach him. People will gather at the dramatic sight (*"coup de rame"* including the sound *"drame"*), as if the action of language were suddenly to be made a spectacle:

> Mais je ne m'arrêterai pas
> Les mots jamais entendus prendront le large
> Ils seront de paille enflammée et luiront dans une cage d'amiante
> Suspendue à l'arbre à devinettes
> (But I shall not stop

> The unfamiliar words will set out to sea
> Made of burning straw they will shine in an asbestos cage
> Hung from the riddle tree) (109)

But the voyage was only predicted, and before the end, the scene once again shifts to waiting, to dreams disappointed (*"voiliers éteints"* = extinguished sailboats) or at least reduced in size, like the tiny sailboat on the puddle at the end of "Le Bateau ivre":

> La lettre que j'attends sera de la couleur des voiliers éteints. . . .
> Qu'elle est de petites dimensions cette lettre que j'attends
> Pourvu qu'elle ne s'égare pas parmi les grains de poison
> (The letter I wait for will have the color of extinguished sailboats. . . .
> How small it is this letter I am waiting for
> As long as it does not stray among the specks of poison) (110)

Just after a lyric description of the letter's importance—in the news it contains the poet expects to find all he has lost, animals and their sudden metamorphoses, the stones he used to feel a danger to his voyage (*"pour me dépister,"* to throw me off the track), and the lights *"qui bercent les choses irréelles"* (which lull unreal things)—the rapid decrescendo in size is as spectacular as the imagined voyage of flaming straw in all its splendid ambiguity (the riddle-tree). The tiny physical dimensions of the final menace match those of the letter, the still potentially explosive drama of one corresponding to that of the other.

The violent activity or potential activity so frequent within the poem, like the exclamations frequent in Breton's writings (*"On secoue!," "Allo!" "Allons!," "Oh!," "Ah!"*) force the reader's attention as they increase the interior distance. In "Les Attitudes spectrales," the atmosphere of ghostly calm one might have expected from the title is broken by people walking, as by a tramway, a ship, or a car moving at high speed, as at a gallop. In "Sur la route qui monte et qui descend" (in whose title there is already all the motion of ascent and descent), the running flame never stops from the beginning to the end of the poem.

With the exception of these poems from *Le Revolver à cheveux blancs,* the poem that deals most directly with all the phenomena of action is *Fata Morgana,* where the action is no longer purely exterior (as in the poems discussed above), but rather imaginary or dreamed; the bed replaces the carriages and ships of the preceding poems, and the voyage depends on an interior "marvelous":

> Le lit fonce sur ses rails de miel bleu. . . .
> Le lit brûle les signaux il ne fait qu'un de tous les bocaux de poissons rouges
> Il lutte de vitesse avec les ciels changeants
> Rien de commun tu sais avec le petit chemin de fer. . . .
> Le lit brûle les signaux il ne fait qu'un de tous les bocaux de poissons rouges. . . .[7]
> Enfin tout est repris par le mouvement de la mer
> Non le lit à folles aiguillées ne se borne pas à dérouler la soie des lieux et des jours incomparables
>
> (The bed rushes by on its rails of blue honey. . . .
> The bed crashes the signals unites all the goldfish bowls. . . .
> It races with the changing skies
> Nothing at all in common you know with the little railroad. . . .
> The bed crashes the signals unites all the goldfish bowls. . . .
> Finally all is gathered up by the movement of the sea
> No the bed with insane threads does not limit itself to unwinding the silk of incomparable days and places) (184)

The wildness of the needle might refer to the uncontrolled reactions of the train's speedometer as well as to the thread of silk; the latter might be another version of the *fil conducteur* linking marvelous incidents; and finally, the red stop signals through which the imaginary bed/train crashes might be identified with the inseparable series of goldfish bowls, in turn similar to the cages whose bars are on the inside so that one can escape from them. This poem, like many of the most significant poems of Surrealism, is a rebellion against the generally accepted limits of imagination and of life. The reduction of the distance between realms which is the goal of Surrealist theory and language:

> Et les distances peuvent continuer à fondre
> (And the distances can continue to melt) (193)

is, by a typical paradox, the means for the enlargement of experience:

> Je commence à voir autour de moi dans la grotte
> Le vent lucide m'apporte le parfum perdu de l'existence
> Quitte enfin de ses limites
> (I begin to look around me in the grotto
> The lucid wind brings me the lost perfume of existence
> Finally free of its limits) (182)

"Rideau rideau"

Of all the voyages presented or implied in Breton's poems, the most dramatic are these interior, imaginary, *invisible* ones. Penetrating behind (or beyond) the backdrop of the poem itself, they are not even bound by the limits of the poet's words. They reject the frame of the poem entirely, as in the image already quoted:

> Alors des étendues jettent l'ancre se déploient au fond de mon oeil fermé
> (Then great expanses cast anchor range themselves in the depths of my closed eye) (131)[7]

Nor is the poet's vision in any way directed toward the reader; it is rather a spectacle he offers to himself on an interior stage. All the characteristics of Surrealist personality and expression contribute to the poem as spectacle *for the poet,* such as the emphasis on the dream and on its peculiar qualities of multiplication and ambiguity provoked within the atmosphere of the marvelous he creates.

> Je rêve je te vois superposé indéfiniment à toi-même
> (I dream I see you superposed indefinitely upon yourself) (129)
> Avec moi des bustes de cire plus beaux les uns que les autres mais parmi eux méconnaissable s'est glissé un buste vivant
> (Around me wax busts each more beautiful than the next but a living bust has slipped in unrecognizably among them) (200)

Fata Morgana, which is above all a poem of this "merveilleux," shows these particular deformations of the real in many of its parts; it is essentially a theatrical poem:

> Têtes de femmes qui se succèdent sur tes épaules quand tu dors
> (Heads of women succeeding each other on your shoulders when you
> sleep) (189)

Of course, we cannot tell the "real" head from the others, as, in another poem, Breton cannot distinguish between *"toutes ces femmes fausses et vraies"* (all these women true and false). And if we should happen to look beyond the surface of the poem, we cannot tell even where the poet is supposed to be—the poem is not for us, nor is the poet to be our guide there. He and the person whom he addresses are able to recognize each other:

> C'est toi c'est moi à tâtons sous l'éternel déguisement
> (It is you it is I groping under the eternal disguise) (190),

but to us only the disguise is apparent. Breton seldom lets us forget the décor of the poem, or the fact that we see it, as it were, secondhand: that is, we are obviously looking at his deformed (or marvelous) conception of the scenery. The confusion is further complicated in the setting of the alchemical theater, since—within the obscurity of the occult—even the poet is not completely sure of the true: (*"et c'est vrai ou presque,"* and it is true or almost):

> Il arrive que le regard errant sur les dormantes eaux du fossé circulaire
> Surprenne en train de se jouer le progrès hermétique
> Tout de feinte et dont on ne saurait assez redouter
> La séduction infinie. . . .
> Tout ce qui vient à souhait est à double face et fallacieux
> Le meilleur à nouveau s'équilibre de pire. . . .
> Ceci dit la représentation continue
> Eu égard ou non à l'actualité
> (It happens that the look as it wanders over the sleeping waters of the
> circular ditch
> Surprises hermetic progress taking place.

In complete pretense and whose infinite seduction
Cannot be feared enough. . . .
All that has been wished for is double-faced fallacious
The best again is balanced by the worst. . . .
This said the representation goes on
Whether it takes account of actuality or not) (192–93)

An early poem, "Allotropie," is a prefiguration of the later theatrical
poems; opening, like *Nadja,* with a question of identity, it then presents
the dramatic outline of an ambiguous shadow, perhaps of Breton who is
both guilty and victimized, both disguised and apparent in the permanent contrasts of Surrealist spectacle:

Qui es-tu
Ombre de malfaiteur sur les grands murs
Ombre de signalisateur qui va plus loin que le signal
Je suis le principal coupable
En même temps que le principal innocent. . . .
Quel maquillage
Nul me reconnaîtra
(Who are you
Shadow of evildoer on the great walls
Shadower of signaler going farther than the signal
I am the guiltiest
And at the same time the most innocent. . . .
What makeup
No one will recognize me)

Finally, two poems from *Le Revolver à cheveux blancs* show clearly,
with strong emotional overtones, the split between subject and object
of vision, or between Breton spectator and character in the drama. The
remarkable "Rideau rideau," a brief theatrical-poetic autobiography,
shows Breton's life *played out* on stages while he hisses at it from a
prompter's box that is also a prison, sometimes screaming, sometimes
attempting suicide, feeling himself at once separated from the scene
and involved enough to re-experience the mental crises within the
scenes:

> Mais c'étaient des pays dans lesquels je m'étais perdu
> (But those were countries where I had lost myself) (99)

A man masked with the poet's features and free, as he himself is not initially, wanders up and down; when suddenly the complete liberty *of dream* is granted to the poet, so that he can chase away all the *"apparences réelles,"* the *real* appearances which form his paradoxical universe, the poem ends in an atmosphere of catastrophe absent from the earlier poem. Silhouetted against the white wall of the basement, surrounded by the aura of the *merveilleux,* appears the poet's other self, outlined in fire and with a bullet piercing his heart. Once more, he is the criminal and the victim, in his own theater.

The positive equivalent of both these poems, and the possible key to their significance (as Breton would say) is the famous "Vigilance," a dream poem where the poet sets fire to his own dreaming body (that is, he *dreams* of setting fire to his own body as he dreams, in an endless, or marvelous, circle) in a mood of peace, quiet, and resolve; in this scene he is purified by the patient beaks of the birds of fire and at last, leaving behind him all the heavy, material, and human dross, enters the ideal ark of the universe. No longer guilty, or innocent, since he is not now judged by human standards, he is granted a paradisiacal vision of the center of things and finally possesses the connecting link he has sought so long: *"Je tiens le fil"* (I hold the thread). Here the poet identifies himself with the alchemist and with the matter on which the alchemist works, with the unpurified and then with the purified, as well as with the agent of the purification. Tzara's *Homme approximatif* undergoes a similar purification by fire and *transmutation* after his long voyage. In both cases, poet and poem, actor and spectacle unite beyond the framework of literature. More than any other, this is the experience of Surrealist poetry.

"Une fois surtout une fois"

> C'en est fait du présent du passé de l'avenir
> Je chante la lumière unique de la coincidence
> (The present past future are finished
> I sing the unique light of coincidence) (139)

The hourglasses and clocks occasionally present in Breton's early poems play very little part in his later poems. The sails of the boat in "La

Mort rose" are made of "his one day hour by hour," but the nature of the Surrealist vision with its perpetual balance prevents any emphasis on the *development* of time. As Breton remarks in his attack on novelistic descriptions, it is better not to speak at all about the *"moments nuls"* of one's life, the totally insignificant periods. The usual attitude of Surrealism depends on a conviction that the spectacle is permanent and that one's action upon it is constant. It neither *changes,* nor develops, although it may alternate. The distinction is essential.

If there seems to be a progression from the transient, nonpurified state of raw matter to the purified, eternal state gained by the process of transmutation, it is a progression that must be continually re-created. Just as Breton is forced to refuse the idea of a revolution toward a specific end that, being reached, might then invalidate the idea of further revolution, he must—in order to preserve the continual movement of the Surrealist gesture—insist on the cyclical nature of all Surrealist action:

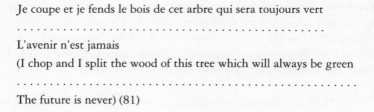

> Je coupe et je fends le bois de cet arbre qui sera toujours vert
>
> . . . .
>
> L'avenir n'est jamais
>
> (I chop and I split the wood of this tree which will always be green
>
> . . . .
>
> The future is never) (81)

One never arrives at the future, and yet it controls many of the visions within the poems ("Rendez-vous," "La Mort rose," "Les Attitudes spectrales"), and occasionally, as in the poem just quoted, the situation presented would only be possible in that future which is never supposed to be.

> Les rideaux qui n'ont jamais été levés
>
> Flottent aux fenêtres des maisons qu'on construira
>
> (The curtains which have never been raised
>
> Flutter in the windows of the houses yet to be built) (81)

No prejudice from the past weighs down the present, nor does the present limit the future, which will never be sufficiently tangible to disprove prophecies or interfere with dreams. All the tenses of Surrealism coincide in a complete liberty:

La vie comme un passeport vierge

(Life like a virgin passport)

By the stubborn denial of chronological separation, the full dualistic intensity of any particular moment can be felt, and can be felt as eternal:

A la vie à la mort cours à la fois les deux lièvres

Cours ta chance qui est une volée de cloches de fête et d'alarme

(For life for death chase both rabbits at the same time

Take your chance which is a pealing of bells of celebration and alarm)

(162)

A la vie à la mort ce qui commence me précède et m'achève

(For life for death what begins precedes me and finishes me) (189)

The Surrealist attitude is as concrete as any other: a certain tree-lined square exists so that we can cross it at a certain angle *"dans la vraie vie"* (in real life), and in the forest seen right at this moment through the window, *if we had the key,* we would find the only clearing important for us. It is true that in an early poem of *Poisson soluble,* Breton expresses a certain *ennui* at the interchangeability of hours, persons, and events:

Ce Monsieur, vous ne le connaissez pas? c'est

M. Lemême. Je vous présente Madame Madame . . .

Nous y sommes: l'ennui, les belles parallèles,

ah! que les parallèles sont belles sous la

perpendiculaire de Dieu

(You don't know this man?

it's Mr. Thesame. May I present Mrs. Mrs. . . .

Here we are: tedium, the beautiful parallels,

oh! how beautiful the parallels are under

the perpendicular of God) (56)

And in "Le Verbe être" he laments the despair of four o'clock, of midnight, of the everlasting sameness of experience:

C'est une corvée de jours de moins qui va

encore faire ma vie

(one day less upon another is going to
make up my life again) (86)

Nevertheless, in the later poems, the combination of unique and interchangeable finds its resolution in the profoundly optimistic theory already
touched on, concretized in the phrase "Toujours pour la première fois":

Toi que je découvre et qui restes pour moi toujours à découvrir[9]
(You whom I discover and who remain for me always to discover) (145)

All the moments are new within the unique love to which these lines
refer, within the Surrealist paradise, where, since evil does not exist, the
apple tree is no longer an agent of damnation: "Tout le pommier en fleur
de la mer/All the apple tree flowering with sea."

According to Breton, the task of the Surrealist poet is to help us
understand that *"le phénix/est fait d'éphémères"* (that the phoenix is made of
ephemerids), that the marvelous phenomenon of rebirth does not necessarily imply the phenomenon of ennui—for the moments, which do not
last, are fresh, unique, never the same, even if they are at the same time
eternal. No more revealing study of the Surrealist spirit can be under-
taken than the study of the endings of Breton's poems. Almost every one
displays what would be traditionally called a perfect ending, suited
exactly to the mood of the poem or to its themes or images, and yet
from each ending the entire poem, or another unique and yet similar,
could begin afresh. Thus, for example, the poem that begins *"Toujours
pour la première fois"* ends with the same line, and yet, according to the
sense of the poem, it is no longer the same line.[10] I take this as a key
poem, like *The Key to the Fields.*

Fata Morgana, the poem that best illustrates the importance Breton
accords to the interior voyage, to the unique moment of perception, to
the constant *play* and the spectacle of the marvelous:

C'est la pièce sans entr'acte le rideau levé une fois pour toutes sur la cascade
(It's the play with no intermission the curtain raised once and for all on
the cascade) (185)

is, just as clearly, the poem of Surrealist hope that goes far beyond a
fairy tale.

> Ce matin la fille de la montagne tient sur ses genoux un acordéon de
> chauves-souris blancs
> Un jour un nouveau jour . . .
> (This morning the mountain girl holds on her knees an accordion of
> white bats
> A day a new day . . .) (179)

The motif *"un nouveau jour"* is repeated, and every time it is new. Love does not lose in not changing its visage, Breton reiterates here, nor does life; they are always seen for the first time, no matter when. The luxurious spectacle *watched* by the people who remain *"dans les ombres du décor"* (in the shadows of the scenery) to contemplate a great feast contrasts vividly with the total simplicity and emotion of the poem's end, in which the poet is involved:

> . . . Plus ne m'est rien rien ne m'est plus Oui sans toi
> Le soleil
> (. . . Nothing means anything to me to me nothing means Yes without
> you
> The sun) (195)

The final image of the sun answers the initial image of the morning, the love denies the distance of the *spectacle,* and the poet-hero,

> Un homme grand engagé sur un chemin périlleux
> Cet homme parmi tant d'autres brusquement semblables
> (A tall man started on a perilous path
> This man among so many others suddenly similar) (188),

does not this time force the reader outside his own theater.

Finally, it is on the sense of the unique encounter as eternal that the poetic structure of Breton's Surrealism is based. This is the key to all the fields and the resolution of all the dualities inherent in the Surrealist attitude. And it is at this point that the transmutation of spectator into participant could begin:

> Tu verras l'horizon s'entrouvrir . . .[11]
> (You will see the horizon start to open . . .) (71)

Chapter Ten
1945: Arcane 17

A gap in the dream. Does it mean that nothing is ever found again? But this distressing certainty calls immediately for another to compensate for it, even better, to reconcile the mind with the first, and this second certainty is that nothing is ever lost.

—Arcane 17, 144

Nadja opened with a question of identity, *Communicating Vessels* with a meditation on the dream; *Arcane 17* opens with a straightforward statement where both are assumed, and neither discussed: "In Elisa's dream. . . ." A "real" woman and the "real" landscape of the Gaspé Peninsula form the background for the book, in which the soliloquy on anarchy and on the true "adventures of the mind" (those adventurers who refuse both *"le pli"* of traditions and the patina of institutions) takes second place to the descriptions of love as a perfect union of existence and essence. It is now for Breton the profound and all-inclusive human counterpart of the sublime point and the marvelous image, a union so luminous that either of its elements seen without the other "appears to be the result of a dissociation, a dislocation of one single block of light" (*A,* 39).

Arcane 17, a book in praise of the esoteric, is nevertheless filled with images of light, transparency, incandescence ("this luminous point," *A,* 19; "incandescent points," *A,* 22; "this flame," "the window unveils itself," *A,* 121; "all the lights prepare to communicate," *A,* 75), these befitting Breton's rediscovery of personal happiness and a concurrent faith in the possible "Resurrection" of all things from their state of melancholy and apparent death:

> Yes, the highest thoughts, the noblest feelings can experience a collective decline, and also the human heart can break and books can get old and everything must die on the exterior, but a power in no sense supernatural makes even of this death the condition for renewal. It guarantees as a preliminary all the exchanges which see to it that nothing precious is lost on the interior, and that through the obscure metamorphosis, from season to season, the butterfly will take on again his exalted colors. (*A,* 128–29)

Even the stagnant pond described in these pages comes to life as the waves sweep across it. This is the poetic faith, and Breton assures us that its true place is never *in* the world, but somewhat removed from the place of action, that the "fields of discovery" to which he so often refers are interior. The Resurrection, like the Rebellion he encourages, carries its justification *in itself* and cannot be disappointed by events extrinsic to it. The latter, insofar as the world is influenced by what Breton calls the "masculine mind" in its rational state, can only be redeemed by the fertile *anima* or the irrational feminine mind as it is expressed in poetry and art. Here Breton states his faith in a "terrestrial salvation by woman."

In the face of the intransigence of the rational, which has produced the most sterile and the cruelest of worlds, Breton invokes her always powerful cry of "refusal and alarm," her insistence on the brotherhood of man, and her warning about the dangers of nationalism. For him, woman is at once the Morning Star ("the star is upon you"), Lucifer the Light-Bearer, Eve, and the individual woman illuminating the individual man: "When fate brought us together, the greatest shadow was in me and I can say that it is within me that this window was opened" (*A,* 105). Above all she is Mélusine. Both mermaid and woman, child and adult, sister to the alchemists and their ideal mistress, Mélusine in her marvelously dual nature is the heroine of the most "splendid myth" of Surrealism. "I choose the child-woman, not to oppose her to the other woman, but because in her and only in her does the other prism of vision seem to dwell in absolute transparency" (*A,* 198).[1] In spite of all the magical transformations, she is always like herself; she proves the permanence of the miracle: "For Mélusine, before and after the metamorphosis, *is* Mélusine" (*A,* 92).

From his ideal point on the Rocher Percé (although he takes pains to state that "everything" prevents him from being, even there, the ideal observer), Breton salutes not only the double nature of woman and the extraordinary luminosity of human love in spite of its myriad deceptions, but the more general "fragility" and "magnificence of the human gift." Finally he invokes the alchemical work (or the *arcane work*) that touches the poetic genius and the poetic life in its *play* of opposites ("this atrocious emptiness replacing without the least transition the fullness of the heart"), which the dual nature of Mélusine perfectly fits. The hidden regions where the alchemical work transforms the opposites into a crystalline union can be explored only by poetry, and only the poet aided by his *soror* has access to them, for it is in her eyes that they are completely revealed. In describing his mental anguish and his struggle to "recover the poetic understanding of the universe beyond the great pity of the epoch and my own confusion," Breton pays the highest possible tribute to the woman whose "grandeur" saved him from despair. He is able now to reiterate his faith in "love, but only as between two beings it rises to the invulnerable," in art, "but only art in its supreme solicitations and the struggle to the bitter end for liberty" (*A*, 81).

Arcane 17 is not a retreat from the image of *Les Vases communicants*, but its double. At a certain point of the day, Breton remarks, "It is done: all the lights communicate" (*A*, 76).

Chapter Eleven

1953: *The Key to the Fields*

Breton was always interested in the people he saw as "bearers of keys." They are endowed with a power of *opening* various possibilities for others, with a strength of desire and of dialectical wisdom to be envied: Giordano Bruno was, for Breton, one of the great bearers of keys for his philosophical dialectics. Breton saw the sensual visionaries he loved, like the Spanish Góngora, for example, as carrying these keys on their long traverse of poetry and the world.

In spite of the number, the chronological range, and the apparently diverse subjects of these essays, the central theme here is more closely defined than in earlier collections. One would not say, of course, that they were written in strict adherence to an *a priori* topic, but that at this point the forcefulness of the Surrealist attitude is such as to convey not only an intensity of feeling, but an actual coherence of theme and structure. Taken together, the essays of this collection comprise a convincing statement on the Surrealist revolution—on its rejection of the world as given, on the means it advocates for enlarging and conveying the Surrealist poetic vision (the adjectives being treated as strict equivalents by Breton), and on its aim of re-creating the world and simultaneously, the human understanding.

Disorientation

"Before the Curtain," Breton's commentary on the Surrealist exhibition of 1947, is an impassioned defense of the group's attitude, which he defines as "the *great disorientation,* no longer in a limited space like a game of blindman's buff, but in all space and in all time, without keeping the least point of reference" (*CC,* 90). This is, he says, the same attitude that the Surrealists had recommended in front of the blank page: a total throwing-off of any past—of memory, of knowledge, of proven talent—for a total future liberty of inspiration granted *spontaneously.* He adopts for a motto a formula created by the Roumanian Surrealists—*"La connaissance par la méconnaissance"* (knowledge through miscomprehension)—and calls for the "categorical refusal of the conditions of life and thought inflicted on man in the middle of the twentieth century" (*CC*, 91), a refusal that implies a certain ascetic strength, as he freely admits. In a footnote to this passage he emphasizes that this attitude is the exact opposite of that adopted by some former members of the Belgian Surrealist group, gathered around the painter René Magritte, who made a decision to let into their works only "charm, pleasure, sun, desirable objects" to the exclusion of anything that signified "sadness, anguish, threatening objects." Even if this was a desperate measure on their part to conform to the resolution of a political group to whose orders they were committed, it would be hard not to compare such a decision to that of a child who might decide to immobilize the needle of the barometer at "fair" to keep the weather good. Already ten years earlier, the famous essay "The Marvelous against Mystery" (which opens *La Clé des champs*), pitting *le merveilleux,* that is, the Surrealist marvelous, against *le mystère,* that is, all other senses of the mysterious, begins with the same "refusal of life as it is given to us."

Nonacceptance is the starting point of Surrealism, as of Dada; whether it is considered a purely negative phenomenon or the initial impulse for a positive program, this point cannot be overlooked at any stage. Built into any theory acceptable to Surrealism, it guarantees that enough flexibility be maintained for a constant questioning. One of the most moving and most revealing statements Breton ever made was that when the attitudes of Surrealism had themselves become unacceptable, he would be the first to align himself with the successor to Surrealism. It is less important to debate whether in fact Surrealism did or will become "out of date" than to recognize the genuine feeling behind his statement.

In "The Mechanic," an essay on the stories of Jean Ferry, Breton honors all the works "electrified by this need of subversion"[1] that the individual is obliged to demonstrate against the evidence of a general "domestication." If, however, the means used to subvert are poor, the attempt will be gravely compromised. The *scandal* presented by the world grows from day to day, and the Surrealist must bear witness to it in a properly Surrealist fashion, must be careful not simply to borrow methods from other "movements" whose range and potentiality will not suffice for the peculiar intensity of the Surrealist revolution. The primary weapon of subversion recommended in "The Mechanic" is that of the dream, which will both undermine the pinnings of the "active" world and redeem it. Breton seconds Ferry's invitation to "cultivate the dream, to make it produce all it can by any means whatsoever and especially by the most 'difficult' means" (221). Surrealism is never to be "easy," rather the exact opposite; the Surrealists take a perfectly justified pride in the difficulty, even the obscurity, of their theories and their creations, both for its own sake and as a defiance of what they judge to be the superficial, nonrevolutionary facility of the non-Surrealist posture.

The title essay of the collection attacks Christianity, rationalism, and art criticism as the three elements that have been responsible for the sheeplike and ineffably dull character of the public mind. But even the tone of the title is completely positive: "The Art of Madmen, the Key to the Fields." Being without rational constraint or purpose, the insane man ("*le fou*") is in a state of liberty never felt before except in the primitives, who also have their own structures, which Breton considers less oppressive than ours. The art of the "insane"[2] cannot be appreciated within the narrow boundaries that logic usually confines us, so we, the public, must enjoy the art before trying to "understand" it, and the critics should do the same. Contemplation of such art has the salutary effect of planting in our minds the seeds of *doubt*, "this healthy doubt which will open the path of a superior and serene intelligence" (221).

The Marvelous and the Open

All the essays of this collection, insisting as they do on what is termed in the first one "a rejection of the real world which can only end with this world," urge a simultaneous "law of pure and simple abandonment to the *marvelous*, in this abandonment residing the only source of eternal communication between men" ("The Marvelous against Mystery"; *CC*, 8, 12). The marvelous is not to be confused with the mysterious, which is *sought* and is therefore the sign of a weakness and a lack. The latter can be the product of work and effort, while the former is a matter of passion, like love. One succumbs to it rather than choosing it; it is of necessity spontaneous rather than calculated. The link between this notion of the marvelous and the value set on dreams, on revelations of chance and of automatic procedures, and on the mind of the mentally abnormal is clear. In all these cases, the "seers" or listeners[3] renounce the "critical intelligence of their acts. Lucidity is the great enemy of revelation" (*CC*, 10). In such a context, Breton's hesitation to cut open some Mexican jumping beans (in the company of the psychoanalyst Lacan and others) to see what was really inside is particularly interesting.

For him, as he explains in "Fronton-Virage," knowledge instantly impairs the sense of wonder and *stops* the possibility of deliberation within the human mind. Therefore, it is, in "marvelous" situations, to be

avoided as long as possible. Breton contradicts the version recounted by
Caillois and Etiemble, both of whom claimed he refused ever to open the
beans. His philosophy is not *"obscurantiste,"* he says:

> I *insist* on this nuance characteristic of my way of thinking . . . that they
> would not be opened until we had exhausted the discussion about the
> *probable* cause of the movements. . . . I was in no way opposed to this
> investigation and if I wanted to delay it a bit, I still considered it neces-
> sary. It is obvious that the idea I held and continue to hold of magic
> would have kept me from wanting to "save" it so cheaply. We were after
> all adults: I restricted myself to the demand that the mind be used more
> seriously before calling on the flat testimony of the eyes. (186)[4]

In the place of a *closed rationalism* and a *closed realism,* which are unitary
concepts, Breton recommends the *open rationalism* and *open realism*
described by the philosopher Gaston Bachelard.[5] The means of opening
our theories and our minds are identical to those he calls the "key to the
fields," the fictional and the imaginary. Fiction, the counterforce to the
world of the real, is the realm in which we must locate a new collective
myth appropriate for our epoch, as the Gothic novel was for the nine-
teenth century. All the "electric" currents it carried (miraculous appari-
tions, and what Breton calls the *light* of overwhelming coincidence) are
more alive than ever and are waiting to be embodied in the new form we
must elaborate. A collective sensitivity, an arousal of consciousness as of
life (*"prise de conscience* commune *de la vie"*) is necessary for the general liberation of the modern mind (*"Not Limits, Frontiers of Surrealism"*).
     In the essay "As in a Wood," Breton quotes Malcolm de Chazal's the-
ory of the night as a key to open things (*"clé d'ouverture"*) in that it is able
to vanquish all the logical antinomies; these antinomies haunt
Surrealism, which seeks to overcome them and still preserve the tension
they create. Breton had given a lyrical description of them in the first
essay of the collection, explaining that since they had existed prior to our
social system, they are not likely to disappear even when it does:

> These antinomies should be overcome because they are felt as cruel, in
> that they also imply a slavery, but one more definitive and deeper than
> temporal slavery, and this suffering, like the other, must not find man
> resigned to it. These antinomies are those of waking and sleeping (reality
> and the dream), reason and madness, the objective and the subjective,
> perception and representation, the past and the future, the collective
> sense and love, and of life and death themselves. (*CC,* 18)

For Breton, as he explains in "As in a Wood," the cinema is the most obvious and general fiction possible, the "only absolutely modern mystery." ("Mystery" has here the medieval sense of general public celebration as well as its more usual sense; Breton mentions explicitly that one goes to the cinema as one might a church.) A film brings about a total *disorientation* from the real, daytime world, and yet links that world to the world of night (or the imagination). It is itself a highly developed *"clé d'ouverture"* because it encourages the mechanism of correspondences on which all Surrealist realizations depend for their range and their depth.

A more primitive form of mystery is the "halo" seen by the Surrealists around certain objects created by less "civilized" peoples. These objects stimulate the poetic (Surrealist) view of things, which is characterized by its triumph over the dualities of perception and representation, of the physical and the mental. Incarnations of the "poetic sublime," they offer us brief and startling glances toward *"something else"* that we cannot know by our intelligence alone ("Oceania").

Poetry and art are both to some extent refutations of the book and the theater. "I am not afraid to say that Surrealism attacked the sense of the book itself." (*CC,* 64). Breton is now convinced, even though he had collaborated in the writing as well as in the presentation of early Surrealist (and Dada) plays, that the theater, like literature, is often slow to act on the modern imagination, that it is less easily electrified with subversive tendencies. For him, writings of Valéry and of Proust are invalidated by their nonrelevance to the moment; Apollinaire, in spite of his enormous gifts, his sense of intellectual adventure, and his realization that it was still necessary to "disturb the very essence of the word" (*"toucher à l'essence du Verbe"*), was betrayed by his determination to celebrate France's participation in World War I (relevant, perhaps, but mistaken in Breton's view).

Breton propounds the above ideas in his speech to the French students at Yale in 1942 (called "Situation of Surrealism Between the Two World Wars"); he rejoices at the demise of so-called rationality and tells them of the Surrealist faith in the *"genius* of youth." He also makes a detailed résumé of Surrealist theory in its advocacy of dialectical processes (those of Heraclitus, Meister Eckhart, and Hegel; Surrealism is, as the reader will have already noticed, as eclectic as it is impassioned), Surrealism, in this view, advocates an almost medieval community of spirit, constantly revising its methods of knowledge to include each new revelation of the unconscious, from automatism to the associated reliance on chance events as "manifestations of exterior necessity clearing a path in the human unconscious," so reconciling human beings and the external world. The humor it calls black serves as an escape valve for the disillusionment provoked by the world insofar as it is still unrevolutionized. Above all, says Breton, Surrealism has succeeded, even as it expresses the anguish of its time, in giving a "new configuration to *beauty*" (*CC,* 73).

Analogy and Necessity

Two essays of 1947 serve as the basis for a Surrealist criterion of style and of judgment: "Rising Sign" is an extensive elaboration of the Surrealist conviction that nothing is gratuitous, that everything demonstrates a certain necessity that can always be deciphered if only we know the code. Not only are things exterior to us linked to each other, but we are linked to them in ways that our conscious mind is unable to comprehend. The experiences of objective chance (*"le hasard objectif"*), a general term that includes the specific discoveries of found objects and expressions called *"objets trouvés"* (found objects), *"trouvailles"* (findings) and automatic writing, speaking, and drawing, show the more personal correspondences between our predictions and our future, our hidden desires and their unexpected fulfillment, which we might not otherwise have recognized. Any method is valuable if it leads to the production of an analogy, which Breton describes as the

> spontaneous, extra-lucid, insolent relationship which is established, under certain conditions, between one thing and another that common sense would never think of bringing together. (*CC,* 111)
> The primordial contacts have been cut: these contacts, I say, that only the analogical impulse succeeds fleetingly in reestablishing. Whence the importance assumed, at distant intervals, by these brief and infrequent sparklings of the lost mirror. (*CC,* 113)

Bringing two things together into a previously untried juxtaposition is the surest way to develop new vision, a new language, and thus a new universe that would never have been visible within the *sequential* framework of ordinary logical perception and expression (A,B,C,D,E . . .). Surrealists know how to place A with E, never concerning themselves with what should precede or follow what; all elements are seen as simultaneous.

"Surrealist Comet" lists as the first article of the Surrealist program: "to maintain plastic expression in a state of incessant potential recreation in order to translate human desire in its constant fluctuation." It is not only flexibility and energy of style that matter, it is also the community of experience and expression. To be sure, the forms of collective desire are scattered as well as highly individualized, but they can be made to converge at the point of a new myth, the existence of which serves to confirm the "indivisible Surrealist pact between humans," in Breton's phrase. He once again mentions the beings or objects *"à halo,"* with the aura of the sacred about them, and demands a specific *initiation* by poetry or art to the universe toward which they gesture.

And it is here that the initial step in the Surrealist program—"the great disorientation"—leads clearly to its end, in the sense of its purpose. Against the traditional pose of both painters and street merchants, their hands on their hips like people in the form of jugs (a fatalistic pose signifying the keeping of the status quo while waiting for a better world), Breton shouts: "Enough jug-men." Surrealism's absolute rejection of both the *realistic* and the *abstract* is of a moral order rather than an aesthetic one:

> Non-Surrealist and, to our way of thinking, regressive, is any work turned toward the daily spectacle of beings and things, that is, participating immediately in the animal, vegetable, and mineral furniture which surrounds us even if the latter should be rendered optically unrecognizable by being "deformed." The Surrealist work banishes resolutely anything in the realm of *simple* perception, whatever intellectual speculation is grafted on it to modify appearances. If the jug remains enemy number one here, it is understood that the Surrealist means to put in the same sack the little ship, the bouquet of anemones, and the obliging lady who used to pose either dressed or naked. (*CC,* 100)

Abstract art, on the other hand, represents an abdication of human desire and a rupture of the precious human perception and thought that Surrealism would like to reconcile. The criterion of Surrealist art is not, as is often thought, any particular technique, but rather the spirit in which it was conceived[6]—it is for this reason that Surrealism can be seen as a movement of genuinely moral intent. The end of each of Breton's essays is strong, from that point of view especially. In this one, he gives a summary, brief and poetic, of the triple goal that it is the *honor* of the Surrealist poets and artists to fulfill insofar as it is possible: "to bring about a social liberation, to work unceasingly for the complete removal of the accumulated encrustations imprisoning our customs, and to reconstruct human understanding dramatically" (*CC,* 105).

   The recurrent appeal of all these essays is to passion and to the spirit of youth as its ideal embodiment. The old rationalistic world has again and again proved the emptiness of its values, which have led only to war and to unhappiness. Revolt is inseparable from generosity, individual creation and understanding from collective feeling, in the overall task of promoting a "libertarian" world ("some say a Surrealist world, but it is the same" ["The Bright Tower," *CC*, 273]). The best description of the re-created world is that promised by the alchemist ("Behold, I shall renew all things" ["Fronton-Virage"]), a world into which one is finally initiated in an extreme step that "leads the self beyond any conditioned state whatsoever."[7] That the Surrealists should think such a transcendence of our ordinary human conditions possible is perhaps proof of their irrationality. But since it is precisely on that going beyond "normality" and reason that their revolution is based, the criticism is not seen by them as negative, but rather as a positive testimony to the unity of their motives and their way of expressing them. Their words are addressed to the young, who will understand them, and to the passionate, who will agree with them.

Chapter Twelve
1965: *Surrealism and Painting*

Changing sight: one of the ways to satisfy a far more wide-reaching ambition, because it is nothing less than *changing life.*[1]

Breton's essays on art, first published in 1928 as *Surrealism and Painting* (the definitive and larger edition dates from 1965), share with all his work a style of passionate conviction and a lyricism rarely surpassed in the French language. Their interest depends little on one's acquaintance with the particular artists about whom Breton is writing—strangely, and bearing witness to the strength of Breton's own personality, many of the descriptions seem interchangeable from artist to artist. We learn a great deal more about Breton's viewpoint than about the subjects of his gaze and discourse. He seems more to be thinking of the subject matter, sometimes extrapolating from it a larger concern, than to be *looking* at the paintings.

Expectation

Plastic art, like fiction, is an ideal setting for the "great disorientation" on which Surrealism depends, for the sense of a *"modern disturbance"* it incarnates. At its best it can have the same socially *isolating* effect as the works of Lautréamont, Rimbaud, Mallarmé, separating the human mind from traditional backgrounds: "the words family, country, society, seem to us macabre jokes" (*SP*, 15). Nor is the isolating effect merely a social one. Breton recounts the power certain canvases have always held over him; he feels himself lost in the space between their frames, their reality overcoming not only the reality of the world beyond them but also his own personal identity. "I lost, without being able to help myself, the sense of my role" (*SP*, 13). To this statement might be added another, which has all the ambiguity of the most celebrated Surrealist aphorisms: "For *we are not,* in literature and in art" (*SP*, 39). The life of the canvas or the page takes over from our life so that we *are* only what it is.

Surrealists live in permanent expectation of experiences, sensations, unwilling to treat anything as a simple object confined to a single purpose and placed in the world for just that purpose. At any point, a revelation could come from the least expected source. "Nothing that surrounds us is an object for us, for us everything is a subject" (*SP,* 59).

On the other hand, it is up to us to make of the nonfictional world a work of art. Everything is affected by our gaze upon it; for the Surrealists, it is of ultimate importance to realize that interior desire controls vision. Hamlet's clouds were not *like* animals, they *were* animals, says Breton, since Hamlet saw them that way. "There are no landscapes. Not even a horizon" (*SP,* 68). Our own thoughts surround the physical, dominating it completely. If this seems to contradict certain of the above statements, such uncomfortable ambiguity is characteristic of Surrealism. We are masters, by our imagination, of the exterior universe. We are by the same token subject to our own imagining of it, and to that of the artists whose vision we cannot help but share, in a sort of double servitude that is also a double mastery of reality:

> Figures of our suspicion, beautiful sad shadows who surround our cavern, we know that you are shadows. The *great subjective light* inundating the canvases of Tanguy is the one which leaves us the least alone, in the least deserted place. There is no creature here who does not participate metaphorically in the life we choose to live, who does not answer the expectation which is ours . . . (*SP,* 69)

Breton insists that in Tanguy's paintings, to take a good case of Surrealist sight, we can perceive very clearly the mental world that is just beginning.

For Breton, paintings must above all not reinforce what we see around us, which would exist nevertheless, for that would be making a pitiful use of the "magic power" of the artist's hand, "an inexcusable abdication." This is in line with his constant exhortations to champion whatever has not been known over what is already all too well acknowledged. In *Break of Day* (*PJ,* 150), he praises the revolutionary—in fact, revolutionizing—power of the artist to "confront whatever already exists with everything that could exist, to pull from what has never yet been seen everything that can persuade what has already been seen to make itself less visible" (*OC* II, 365). Any work of art must refer to an *interior* model, as the Cubist poet Pierre Reverdy and others believed. Based on the imagination, it must create reality, not preserve it in its usual form. The painter deliberately practices the crime of "*lèse-réalité,*" refusing to permit objects their ordinary associations. When Breton praises Jean Arp, it is for his daring to rearrange the most everyday elements so that they seem to acquire totally new necessities and uses, as do the newly arranged words of the Surrealist language:

> With Arp, the hour of distribution has gone by. The word "table" was a begging word: to write. . . . In reality, if it is now understood what we mean by that, a nose is perfectly at home beside a chair, it even takes on the form of a chair. . . . The birds have never sung better than in this aquarium. (*SP*, 71)

Breton repeatedly emphasizes the courage that is required to undertake his mental adventure. Only the "fever of *total conquest*" could inspire travelers to set out on "the mysterious road where fear awaits us at every step, where the desire we have to turn back is overcome only by the fallacious hope of being accompanied" (*SP*, 16). Certain artists, like Picasso, paint canvases so illuminated that they cast light over the whole path the others must travel; others, like de Chirico, show a purely interior illumination; but all true Surrealist paintings point the way to a "future continent" and manifest a genuine faith that "each person is able to accompany an always more beautiful Alice to some wonderland" (*SP*, 19). The "heroic commitment" of the Surrealist adventure means, for Breton, giving up the evident for the obscure, leaving, that is, the prey for the shadow, forsaking all that is certain and visible for what is uncertain and so far nonexistent except within the realm of the imagination.

Commitment and Connection

As we have already seen, the Surrealist is not permitted to simply turn his back on reality. The temptation by idealism is only temporary: Surrealism goes beyond it toward a dialectical reality, a dramatic and constant interchange between the real and the sur-real or super-real.

> Everything I love, all I think and feel, inclines me toward a particular philosophy of immanence in which surreality is contained in reality itself and is neither superior nor exterior to it. And reciprocally, for the container is also the contained. It is like communicating vessels, between the containing and the contained. (*SP*, 69)

Only by including the real with the unreal can Surrealist paintings possibly meet the final challenge, posed not by a rival kind of art but by the *genuine* anguish of the "real" world. Wonderlands may be aesthetically perfect and still crumble at the test of human suffering. Breton demands that paintings hold good not only when compared with real wheat fields but with famine, which is far more difficult. Surrealists must somehow manage to retain their "noble feelings of discontinuity" (a notion closely related to voluntary disorientation), their aloofness from the human situation and from valuation by others ("we are better than what we *pass for,*" [*SP,* 70]), and yet not lose contact with the non-Surrealist world. As time goes on, the disorientation and aloofness submit more and more to the involvement and moral commitment, but the latter has been unmistakably present to some extent from the beginning.

The "primitivism" of the Surrealist group serves as a criterion for utterly scorning works of art based on historical and civilized visions of the world; however, it offers no excuse for trivial or uncommitted art. It is not the surface arrangement that is questioned, rather something deeper. Max Ernst, for instance, interrogates "the substance of objects, giving it complete licence to determine the shadow, the pose and the form of those objects" (*SP,* 53–54). Ernst understands and undertakes that kind of difficulty that Breton deems an essential part of the heroic commitment to challenge our ordinary perceptions of things "in order to break completely with them, especially with the ease their accustomed aspect shows us." (*SP,* 170). He undertakes the gigantic task of an entire re-creation, bringing with him the pieces of the labyrinth, which cannot be put back together the way they once were: "It was like creation's game of solitaire: all the pieces, unbelievably separated from each other, no longer aware of any particular magnetism one for another, tried to find new affinities" (*SP,* 50). This time everything is reconstituted in *favor of the image,* as in poetry.

On the other side of our own superhuman effort, there is an intense resistance on the part of objects, which adopt attitudes of unrelenting hostility toward each other. To mediate between them, like Ernst, is to be a gambler: "To play all for all. In that resides perhaps the possibility of living for Max Ernst, of living freely, perhaps it is in that that his deep humanity consists" (*SP,* 50).

"Lyricism, characteristic of all the works we admire," has little to do with traditional "lyric" style, referring now not to style, but to vision. When one of these works brings together elements at random, the very possibility that they might have met before fulfills Breton's notion of the lyric. As for the style of Surrealism, it opposes the everyday flatness our eyes are used to witnessing. Surrealist vision is like that of an intelligent and extraordinarily gifted child, its expressiveness not to be betrayed by a dull realism.

Surrealist art does not have to do what non-Surrealist art does; it has no reason to represent what we see or feel, which would be easy enough and takes no special commitment. Surrealism lays down a series of connecting wires (*"fils conducteurs"*) between things not joined before, to make over the world in the image of our interior conception. *Nota bene:* It does not necessarily follow, however, that we will be enticed into every Surrealist canvas we see; the world re-created by certain Surrealists young or old may possibly not fit our vision, or not communicate its own to us. Breton always leaves room for our individual judgment: "Seeing, hearing, is nothing. Recognizing or not recognizing is everything. Between what I recognize and what I do not recognize there is myself. And what I do not recognize, I shall continue not to recognize" (*SP,* 66).

Chapter Thirteen

Freedom

The Real and the Possible

How the "paucity of the real" (as in Breton's "Introduction to the Discourse . . ." about it) strikes with its uncertainty, its terror of the inauthentic: many of the essays in *Break of Day* are permeated by self-doubt.

> Each day I live, each action I commit, each representation that comes to me as if innocently, leads me to believe that I am faking. While writing I go over, like some smuggler at the end of the day, all the instruments destined to the war I wage against myself. (*OC* II, 273)

We well know what Breton never fails to point out, and to point out with a desperate conviction born of knowledge. Here, the reader who has not experienced such a knowledge has only to follow him on faith; the reader who has, is already convinced: "There is, in the knowledge of oneself, only the descent of hell that can lead to apotheosis" (*CC*, 90).

And yet, counterbalancing these moments *without confidence,* Breton's certainty and his faith in his own predictions echo throughout all his work. In *Surrealism and Painting,* as elsewhere, he proclaims in loud tones his ambition as a fighter in the unlimited field of the potential, fighting the easy and domesticated "embroidery" of a world accepted in its limits:

> If some day, I know the time when the terrible struggle of the lived and the livable will end for me, if I have lost all hope of increasing, mightily, the domain of the real in my own actions, until now so terribly limited, if my imagination, shrinking so that it merely coincides with my memory and nothing else, I shall willingly grant myself, as others do, some relative satisfaction. I shall then rank myself with the embroiderers. I shall have forgiven them. But not before then! (*SP,* 13)

Surrealism's long self-comparison, after Rimbaud, to alchemy, should be remembered at this point. For, in the invisibly visible, the alchemical analogy—so stressed as to be taken beyond mere analogy—enters the

thought of Surrealism. In the *Second Manifesto,* Breton proclaims his faith
anew, in the style of *demand* typical of his assertions—he calls for our
attention, and secures it: "I ask . . .," "I demand," "I claim . . .":

> I ask that it be noticed how the goal of surrealist research presents a
> remarkable analogy to alchemical research: the philosophers' stone was to
> permit the human imagination to take a dazzling revenge over all things,
> and here we are once more, after centuries of the domestication of the
> mind and of foolish resignation, trying to set this imagination definitive-
> ly free . . . (*OC* II, 819)

Chapter Fourteen

"There Will Be"

The Future of the Imagination: "Once upon a time
there will be" (1932) *and* "Surrealist Situation of the
Object" (1935)

> The oneiric values have definitively won out over the others and I
> demand anyone be considered a cretin who would still refuse to *see,* for
> example, a horse galloping on a tomato. A tomato is also a child's bal-
> loon, surrealism, I repeat, having suppressed the word "like." The horse is
> about to take on the identity of the cloud, etc. (*OC* II, 301)

Of all the links created or perceived by Surrealism, the one joining imagination and life is unquestionably the most important. More than any
other contemporary writer, Breton devotes his full attention to the elu-
cidation and the celebration of that link. "Once upon a time there will
be," the essay introducing his most widely read collection of poems, *The
White-Haired Revolver,* states the Surrealist creed: *that which is imagined
may someday be.* As the only path to the marvelous and the only remedy
for the desiccation inflicted by the scientific mentality that insists on
stressing the known to the detriment of the unknown, the human imagination must be valued at its proper worth. We have to believe in our
own "suspicions," for they are the real. This belief is not given, it is
rather to be *conquered:* the imagination

> does not have to humble itself before life. . . . There will always be, espe-
> cially among the ideas called accepted and ideas . . . whose acceptance we
> must bring about,[1] a difference capable of making the imagination mis-
> tress of the mental situation. . . .
>   The imaginary is what tends to become the real. (*The White-Haired
> Revolver,* 11)

At this point, Breton speaks of the problem of "the transformation of
energy." We should use all the potential of the imagination; otherwise, it
would be like doing without electricity so the water we had previously

harnessed for electric power could return to a waterfall. This is the main key of *The Key to the Fields*, "A law, pure and simple, of giving oneself over to the marvelous, this abandon containing the single source of eternal communication between humans" (*CC,* 11).

It is all a matter of choice. The Surrealists would choose to initiate us, whenever and wherever possible, to the *poetic process,* the lyric behavior that will give imagination free scope. This procedure, as Breton describes it in his important essay of 1935, "Surrealist Situation of the Object," can be summed up in the following ways.

First, rely less upon the exterior object as such and consider nature "only in its relationship with the interior world of consciousness" (*Manifestes,* 312). Second, examine all the results of the processes we would ordinarily consider arbitrary (for instance, the results of automatic practices or of the "objective chance" that finds us doing certain things without our having planned to). We will, Breton assures us, find the results to be not in the slightest arbitrary, but rather, necessary. The connections between interior and exterior, between subjective and objective, in whatever direction they may seem to move, are *in reality* connections of the marvelous: "What more beautiful star, under what more shining dew, can there ever be woven the cloth stretched from this blue packet to this empty glass?" (*SP,* 28) he asks.

Finally, the poetic imagination must remain free of the weight of logical habits of thought. All true poets must, to this end, persevere in the effort to separate poetry from prose by means of the metaphor. Breton blames the very limited use of the metaphor ("this marvelous instrument") for the "poetic nullity" of the so-called classic centuries of poetry. Free also of seeing any practical end in advance, of any concern for narration, the poet can work for the predominance of the pleasure principle over the reality principle, for the abolition of the *moi* in the *soi,* for the dialectical conciliation of the terms perception and representation. The sense in which the poetic imagination can be called *upsetting* or revolutionary, is that, once having perceived, it calls imperiously for something in the outside world to answer its *prior* interior perception. And, Breton concludes, "[i]t can be predicted that, to a great extent, this something *will be*" (*Manifestes,* 333).

In its turn, moreover, the prediction just quoted is itself an answer to the title of the 1932 essay "Once Upon a Time"; the phrase recurs in a still more positive version eleven years later as part of an interior refrain in the poem "The Estates General": **"there will always be . . . ,"** which is set in a more imposing size of type than the rest of the poem. There will always be moments of ennui, such as the following:

Je ne crois pas que le progrès s'opère dans la direction du sens
La confiance manque
. . . .
J'ai comme un pressentiment de l'asile
Des fuites sans mon éclat personnel
Qui est un peu déchiqueté
(I do not think that progress is made as to meaning
There's no confidence
. . . .
I have a foreboding of the asylum
Escaping without my personal splendor
Which is a little ratty)

The Operation of Poetic Intuition: "About Surrealism in its Living Works" (1955)

. . . the poetry of Césaire, like all great poetry and all great art, is valid at the highest point by the power of transmutation that it puts into play and which consists in producing from the least valued materials, including everything ugly and habitual the philosophers' stone, which, as we know now, is not gold, but freedom itself.[2]

From the philosophers' stone, furthermore, can spring a whole garden of possible settings, each more conducive to the Surrealist image, its finders, and its *adepts*—for such is the tone of longing and lyricism that hovers over the stone. Speaking of Aloysius Bertrand's prose poems called *Gaspard de la Nuit,* Breton claims that

[t]here is no reading after which one cannot continue to seek the philosophers' stone. Humanity has not grown old. In the night of Gaspard, what does it matter if we have to stretch out our hand for a long time to feel one of these very fine rains falling which is going to give birth to some enchanted fountain? (*PP, 99*)

Breton's essay on the state of Surrealism at the moment ("About Surrealism in Its Living Works") considers its accomplishments and its goals from a perspective closer to that of *Arcane 17* than of the earlier essays. In fact, much of his later work lays more stress upon the occultation of Surrealism than upon the poetic work to be done, heard, and understood by all, the latter optimism having been exemplified by the

conclusion of *Communicating Vessels,* when the poets who know how to
fuse the general with the particular will have succeeded

> in obtaining a precipitate of a lovely enduring color. They will already be
> outside, mingled with everyone else in full sunlight, and cast no more
> complicitous or intimate a look than others do at truth itself when it
> comes to shake out, at their dark window, its hair streaming with light.
> (*VC,* 147)

The Surrealist movement had its origin in an operation on language,
Breton explains—language considered not only the expression of unconscious desire (an aspect unduly emphasized because of the exaggerated
interest in automatic writing), but, and from this perspective even more
importantly, the basic matter of creation. In the occult philosophy that
Surrealism admires and emulates, enunciation is at the origin of everything, and therefore, "the name has to *germinate,* so to speak, otherwise
it is false" ("Surrealism in Its Living Works," *Manifestes,* 358). The principal contribution of Surrealism, in poetry as in the plastic arts, is to have
so exalted this germination as to make everything else appear ridiculous.

Here also Breton reiterates Surrealism's attitude toward elective love
as a sufficient negation of the supposed dualism of the soul and the body.
In spite of the difficulties caused by exterior forces of division, the
promise held out by *"l'amour-passion"* is kept. In the world to which it
opens the gates, there is neither sin nor evil.

Third, the Surrealist image, the generator of sparks and the agent of
transparency, is at the same time a proof of the actuality of what Breton
calls elsewhere the sublime point, confirming that "all that is high is like
what is low" and "all that is within is like what is without." The dualities
are overcome and the world becomes less opaque by the poetic operation.

Finally, the *poetic intuition* as it is freed in Surrealism from all its constraints not only assimilates "all of the known forms but creates new
forms" in the processes of generation and germination already described.
Here Breton refers in turn to Schopenhauer, Gérard de Nerval, Charles
Fourier, and René Guénon, in describing various aspects of this mystic
intuition, which is able to "embrace all the structures of the world, manifest or not. It alone provides us with the thread which can lead back to the
path of Gnosis, as knowledge of suprasensible Reality, 'invisibly visible in
an eternal mystery'" ("Surrealism in its Works Alive," *Manifestes,* 363).

Selected Bibliography

SOME PRIMARY SOURCES

(The place of publication is Paris unless otherwise noted.)

1919 *Mont de Piété.* Au Sans Pareil.

1920 *Les Champs magnétiques* (with Philippe Soupault) (reprinted with the plays *Vous m'oublierez* and *S'il vous plaît,* also written in collaboration). NRF, 1968.

1923 *Clair de terre.* Coll. Littérature.

1924 *Les Pas perdus.* NRF (reprinted 1945).
Manifeste du surréalisme, suivi de *Poisson soluble.* Editions Kra.

1928 *Le Surréalisme et la peinture.* NRF (reprinted, with additions and revisions, 1965).
Nadja. NRF (reprinted with revisions, 1963).

1930 *Ralentir travaux* (in collaboration with René Char and Paul Eluard). Editions Surréalistes.
Second manifeste du Surréalisme. Editions Kra.
L'Immaculée Conception (in collaboration with Paul Eluard). Editions Surréalistes (reprinted, Pierre Seghers, 1961).

1931 *L'Union libre.*

1932 *Misère de la poésie—"L'affaire Aragon" devant l'opinion publique.* Editions Surréalistes.
Le Revolver à cheveux blancs. Editions des Cahiers Libres.
Les Vases communicants. Editions des Cahiers Libres (reprinted, NRF, 1955, 1967).

1934 *Qu'est-ce que le surréalisme?* Bruxelles: René Henriquez.
L'Air de l'eau. Editions Cahiers d'Art.
Point du jour (texts from 1924 to 1933). NRF.

1936 *Notes sur la Poésie* (in collaboration with Paul Eluard). G.L.M.

1937 *L'Amour fou.* NRF (reprinted 1945).

1938 *Dictionnaire abrége du surréalisme* (in collaboration with Paul Eluard). Editions Beaux-Arts.
Trajectoire du rêve. Cahiers GLM, no. 7 ("texts concerning the dream," compiled by Breton).
Manifesto Pour un Art Révolutionnaire Indépendant (written in collaboration with Leon Trotsky, signed by Breton and Diego Rivera).

1940 *Anthologie de l'humour noir.* Editions du Sagittaire (last edition, Pauvert, 1966).

105

1941 *Fata Morgana*. Editions du Sagittaire.
1944 *Arcane 17*. New York: Brentano's (reprinted, followed by *Enté d'Ajours*, Editions du Sagittaire, 1947).
1946 *Young Cherry Trees Secured Against Hares/Jeunes Cerisiers garantis contre les lièvres* (bilingual edition of poems). New York: View Editions (reprinted in Ann Arbor Paperbacks, Michigan, 1969).
1947 *Ode à Charles Fourier*. Editions de la Revue Fontaine.
     Yves Tanguay. New York: Editions Pierre Matisse.
1948 *Martinique, charmeuse de serpents*. Editions du Sagittaire.
     Poèmes. NRF (anthology, 1919–48).
1950 *Almanach surréaliste du demi-siècle* (special issue of *La Nef,* numbers 63/64).
1952 *Entretiens 1913–52* (with Andre Parinaud and others). NRF.
1953 *La Clé des champs* (texts from 1937 to 1952). Editions du Sagittaire (reprinted, Pauvert, 1967).
1954 *Farouche à quatre feuilles* (in collaboration with Lise Deharme, Julien Gracq, and Jean Tardieu). Grasset.
1957 *L'Art magique* (with Gérard Legrand). Club Français du Livre.
1961 *Le là. Alès*. P.A.B.
1962 *Manifestes du surréalisme* (including the first and second manifestos, *Poisson soluble,* "Lettre aux voyantes," "Position politique du surréalisme," "Prolégomènes à un troisième manifeste du surréalisme ou non," "Du surréalisme en ses oeuvres vives"). Pauvert.
1970 *Perspective cavalière* (ed. Marguerite Bonnet). Gallimard.
1988 *Oeuvres complètes*, I (ed. Marguerite Bonnet, with Philippe Bernier, Etienne-Alain Hubert, and José Pierre). Gallimard, Editions de la Pléiade.
1992 *Oeuvres complètes,* II (ed. Marguerite Bonnet, with Philippe Bernier, Etienne-Alain Hubert, and José Pierre).

SELECTED SECONDARY SOURCES

(On Breton and Surrealism)

Alexandrian, *André Breton par lui-même*. Seuil: Ecrivains de toujours, 1971.
Alquié, Ferdinand. *Philosophie du surréalisme*. Flammarion, 1955. Thorough, analytic, particularly interesting for the reader who has already some acquaintance with the topic. "Before any critical development, before any reflection on itself, Surrealism proposes to us the hope of existence, and projects this existence in a sort of other world beyond natural life, another world however immanent in it, and seeming to reveal itself to the man who desires to seize the world under the aspect of the marvelous" (15).
Audouin, Philippe. *André Breton*. Gallimard, 1970. Brilliant study.
Balakian, Anna. *Surrealism, the Road to the Absolute*. New York: Noonday Press, 1959; Random House, 1967. Brief discussion of the predecessors of

Surrealism (Baudelaire, Lautréamont, Apollinaire, Reverdy), of the influences upon it (Freud, Hegel), of the Surrealist image and the Surrealist attitude. Surrealism seen as an "earthbound *mystique.*"

―――. *André Breton: Magus of Surrealism.* Oxford University Press, 1971. Clear and positive.

Bédouin, Jean-Louis. *André Breton,* Poètes d'aujourd'hui, Seghers, 1950. Selection of texts with laudatory preface on Breton as a "disturbing meteor."

―――. *Vingt ans de surréalisme, 1939–1959.* Denoël, 1961. Particularly for the more recent period; written by a Surrealist, from the Surrealist point of view.

Béhar, Henri. *André Breton, le grand indésirable.* Calmann-Lévy, 1990.

Bonnet, Marguerite. *André Breton: Naissance de l'aventure surréaliste.* José Corti, 1975. By the knowledgeable and impassioned commentator on Breton, who was the chief editor of the first two Pléiade volumes.

Browder, Clifford. *André Breton, Arbiter of Surrealism.* Geneva: Droz, 1968. "Life and works" study: a bit dry.

Cardinal, Roger, and Robert Stuart Short. *Surrealism: Permanent Revelation.* New York: Dutton, 1970. A good brief study, well illustrated.

Carrouges, Michel. *André Breton et les donneés fondamentales du surréalisme.* Gallimard, 1950. Breton thought this an excellent study. Lofty and eloquent-sentimental style like that of Breton himself. Discussion by a Roman Catholic of Breton's "dialectical humanism," of his image of the crystal, etc.: "that this far-off diamond should grow until it includes the entire universe and how could this be possible if this universe did not burn away all its impurities, if it did not break through all its limits to become a pure sphere of solar crystal?" (87).

Caws, Mary Ann. *Surrealism and the Literary Imagination: A Study of Gaston Bachelard and André Breton.* The Hague: Mouton, 1966.

―――. *The Poetry of Dada and Surrealism: Aragon, Breton, Tzara, Eluard, Desnos. Princeton:* Princeton University Press, 1970.

―――. *The Surrealist Look.* Cambridge: MIT Press, 1996.

―――, ed. with Rudolf Kuenzli and Gwen Raaberg, *Surrealism and Women.* Cambridge: MIT Press, 1991.

Chénieux-Gendron, Jacqueline, *Surrealism.* New York: Columbia University Press, 1990. Translated by Vivian Folkenflik. An intelligent overview.

Cirlot, Juan Eduardo. *Introducción al surrealismo.* Madrid: Revista del Occidente, 1953. "As we have indicated, Surrealism diverges from the dialectical idealism of Hegel inasmuch as it calls for the concrete possession of the world, in its totality and in each one of its parts, spheres, and possibilities" (376).

Crastre, Victor. *André Breton,* Arcanes, 1952. Political point of view: that Breton finally gave up trying to appeal to youth, and that Surrealism came to see that "poetry cannot be made by all in the world we are given" (81). This was its greatest failure. But on the whole, complimentary toward Breton.

Duplessis, Yves. *Le Surréalisme (Que sais-je).* P.U.F., 1950. Arranged by themes; a beginning for the new reader.

Eigeldinger, Marc. *André Breton, essais et témoignages.* Neuchâtel: Baconnière, 1950. A few important essays by Breton, with comments by Gracq, Carrouges, Paulhan, etc.

Fowlie, Wallace. *Age of Surrealism.* Bloomington: Indiana University Press, 1960. A panorama—Lautréamont, Rimbaud, Mallarmé, Apollinaire, Cocteau, Picasso—as well as Breton and Eluard. Some would object to the inclusion of Mallarmé—and particularly of Cocteau—in a book with Breton.

Gershman, Herbert. *The Surrealist Revolution in France.* Ann Arbor: University of Michigan Press, 1968 (and *Bibliography of the Surrealist Revolution in France*). 2 vols. Careful and reliable history, with brief sections on the Surrealist aesthetic, art and Surrealism, etc., accompanied by illustrations, appendixes, and detailed notes. Nicely breezy style; personal, rather critical approach. Breton doesn't come off very well, except as a "publicist."

Gracq, Julien [Louis Poirier]. *André Breton: quelques aspects de l'écrivain.* José Corti, 1948. Concise, intelligent, interesting.

Massot, Pierre de. *André Breton le septembriseur.* José Corti, 1967. Supersentimental.

Matthews, J. H. *An Introduction to Surrealism.* University Park: Pennsylvania State University Press, 1965. Wide-ranging study of themes and techniques in Surrealist art, with frequent and interesting quotations from a variety of spokesmen. Surrealism as an attitude and as a "human mission."

————. *André Breton.* New York: Columbia University Press, 1967. Brief, clear.

Mauriac, Claude. *André Breton, essai.* Editions de Flore, 1949. Thin.

Monnerot, Jules. *La Poésie moderne et le sacré.* Gallimard, 1945. Difficult, abstract. Recommended for advanced readers. "This poetry *opens out on* insanity, but also on the lyric-dialectic, the elaboration of a problematics of existence, impossible possibility, possible impossibility. It opens out on the tragic as on a sort of method which our being would use in order to be" (176).

Nadeau, Maurice. *Histoire du surréalisme.* Seuil, 1954. (Translated in English by Richard Howard as *History of Surrealism*, introduction by Roger Shattuck, Collier, 1967.) This book provokes, because of its title and historical attitude, the wrath of the present Surrealists.

Née, Patrick. *Lire Nadja de Breton.* Dunod, 1993.

Polizzotti, Mark. *Revolution of the Mind: The Life of André Breton.* New York: Farrar, Straus and Giroux, 1994. Definitive study of the life, wonderfully written and authoritative.

Sawin, Martica. *Surrealism in Exile and the Beginning of the New York School.* Cambridge: MIT Press, 1995.

Sheringham, Michael. *André Breton: A Bibliography.* London: Gant and Cutler, 1972.

Tashijian, Dickran. *A Boatload of Madmen: Surrealism and the American Avant-Garde, 1920–1950.* New York: Thames and Hudson, 1994.

Steinmetz, Jean-Luc. *André Breton et les surprises de l'amour fou.* PUF, 1994.

Catalogs and Journal Issues

Yale French Studies. Spring 1964. Surrealism issue.

L'Esprit créateur. Spring 1966. Surrealism issue.

NRF. *André Breton et le mouvement surréaliste.* Special issue, April 1967. See particularly the essays by Andre Pieyre de Mandiargues (on the Surrealist language), Octavio Paz (on revelation, meditation, election), Charles Duits (on the figure of Breton in 1943), Michel Beaujour (on *Nadja*), and Philippe Jaccottet (on the *oratory* nature of Breton's poems).

André Breton Today, ed. Anna Balakian and Rudolf E. Kuenzli. Special issue of *Dada/Surrealism.* New York: Willis Locker & Owens. 1989. With essays by Anna Balakian, Henri Béhar, José Pierre, J. H. Matthews, Michael Riffaterre, Ronnie Scharfman, Jacqueline Chénieux-Gendron, Mary Ann Caws, Margaret Cohen, Michel Beaujour, Rudolf Kuenzli, and others.

Pleine Marge: Cahiers de Littérature, d'Arts Plastiques & de Critique. June 1991. No. 13. "Lire le regard: André Breton et la Peinture." With essays by Dawn Ades, Marie-Paule Berranger, Yves Bonnefoy, Mary Ann Caws, Jacqueline Chénieux-Gendron, Dominique Combe, Isabelle Lorenz, Jean-Michel Rabaté, Michael Riffaterre, Guy Rosolato, Adélaide Russo, Michael Sheringham, José Vovelle.

André Breton, la poésie. Edited by Jacqueline Chénieux-Gendron, no. 1 of *La Revue des Sciences humaines* 237. Lille: Université Charles-de-Gaulle (Lille III), 1995. With essays by Marie-Paule Berranger, Jacqueline Chénieux-Gordon, Jean Decottignies, Gérard Durozoi, Jean-Michel Rabaté, Michael Sheringham, Dominique Viart.

Return of the Exquisite Corpse, for exhibition of the "Cadavre Exquis" at Drawing Center, New York, 1993.

Notes and References

Preface

    1.   "Le temps" is used in the original, meaning both weather and time: Breton and the other Surrealists use all the ambiguities possible.

    2.   André Breton, *Oeuvres complètes,* I, ed. Marguerite Bonnet, avec Philippe Bernier, Etienne-Alain Hubert, et José Pierre, Gallimard, 1988; hereafter cited as *OC* I).

    3.   In deference to the subject of this book, Dada will be discussed in the past tense and Surrealism in the present.

Chronology

    1.   For a reliable and no less fascinating study of Breton's life, see Mark Polizzotti, *Revolution of the Mind: The Life of André Breton.* New York: Farrar, Straus and Giroux, 1995. Hereafter cited as *P.*

    2.   Although it is possible, as Bruce Morrissette suggests in his study, *The Great Rimbaud Forgery: the Affair of "La Chasse Spirituelle"* (St. Louis: Washington University Studies, 1956), that Breton also had a reason "exterior" to the text for suspecting it to be false. He had received, it is said, a phone call warning him of the imposture.

Chapter One

    1.   The spelling is an obvious mockery of such a profession.

    2.   Claude Mauriac, *André Breton,* Editions de Flore, 1949, 345.

    3.   Victor Crastre, *André Breton,* Arcanes, 1952, 194.

Chapter Two

    1.   The numbers in parentheses refer to pages of the book under discussion, in the edition quoted in the Bibliography.

    2.   Breton also quotes Lautréamont's attack against Pascal: "The fly does not reason very well at the present time. A man is buzzing in his ears." (Pascal, in order to show the variability and weakness of the human mind, had said the reverse of this. The Surrealists stand with all that is human, against anything that would seem to depreciate the value or the strength of the imagination.)

    3.   *Conversations: The Autobiography of Surrealism,* trans. Mark Polizzotti (New York: Paragon House, 1992). Hereafter cited in text as *C.* See also Polizzotti's superb biography of Breton.

4. The similarities and differences between Dada and Surrealism are not treated here in any detail, although they are as important as they are interesting. For a brief discussion of them, see Michel Sanouillet, *Dada à Paris* (Pauvert, 1965); Herbert Gershman, *The Surrealist Revolution in France* (Ann Arbor, Mich.: University of Michigan Press, 1968); or my *Poetry of Dada and Surrealism: Aragon, Breton, Tzara, Eluard, Desnos* (Princeton: Princeton University Press, 1970).

5. J. H. Matthews, *The Surrealist Mind* (Selingsgrove: Susquehanna University Press, 1991), 23.

6. Jacqueline Chénieux-Gendron defines a "romantic philosophy" as "a philosophy of being, in which imagination can rediscover Paradise Lost" (*Surrealism,* trans. Vivian Folkenflik, New York: Columbia University Press, 1990), 4.

7. Chénieux-Gendron, 7. See my essay, "Exquisite Essentials on the Cadavre Exquis," *Return of the Exquisite Corpse.* New York: Drawing Center, 1993.

Chapter Three

1. It is this crusading hope that Jules Monnerot describes as the "impossible possible." See *La Poésie moderne et le sacré* (Gallimard, 1945).

2. Symbolist poet Arthur Rimbaud was haunted by the split between the I who speaks and the I who listens as "I speak": *Je est un autre*—I (who is) another, that is, I am, to myself, *the other.*

3. Which are "sadistic" in the strongest meaning of the word, but which are followed in the second part of the work by *Poésies,* the exact opposite of the *Chants:* alternation (as in the Surrealist language of opposites), recantation, forgery, joke? The mystery is unsolved.

4. Because it includes the contraries, on which the whole attitude and style of both movements are based, because it is essentially mobile, and for a number of other reasons. The notion is discussed at length in most of the books on the movements. Of course, during Surrealism's more politically committed periods, the references to dialectic take on a slightly different connotation. During Breton's exile in New York, Meyer Schapiro—fluent in French—invited him for a debate on "dialectic," at which Breton felt himself outargued, after which he used the term less frequently (*P*, pp. 370–76).

5. See the *Lettres de guerre de Jacques Vaché* (Editions Kra, 1949), with four prefaces by Breton (1919, 1924, 1940, 1948). Vaché, an extraordinary personage, at least as Breton describes him, is the inventor of *umour,* spelled just like that (part of the humorous thing). As an example of it, he gives the statement, "IT IS IN THE ESSENCE OF SYMBOLS TO BE SYMBOLIC," and the following definition:

> I think it is a sensation—I was about to say a SENSE—that too—of the theatrical uselessness (and joylessness) of everything. WHEN ONE KNOWS.
> And so that is why enthusiasms—(first of all, they are noisy)—*of others* are hateful. . . ."

And, in another place: "GOD IS ABSURD—for everything is contradictory, right? . . ."

In *his Dada à Paris,* Michel Sanouillet minimizes the great attraction Vaché is supposed to have had for Breton as a myth on Breton's part, invented in order to discount the importance of Tristan Tzara. In any case, the letters of Vaché are illuminating for certain aspects of Breton's early character.

6. "Nous embrassons tout, mais nous n'étreignons que du vent."

7. For example, at the March 1968 exhibition held at the Museum of Modern Art on "Dada, Surrealism, and Their Heritage," there were protests in several newspapers and demonstrations on the spot against the "MUSE-UM/MAUSOLEUM." Parallel accusations were made against the speakers at a "symposium" held in conjunction with the exhibition, on the grounds that to discuss Surrealism within such a setting is to dig its grave, make its autopsy, and so on.

8. Because its "lesson" was that the French nation should have more children. Both the appeal to nationalism and to motherhood were judged abhorrent from the Dada/Surrealist point of view.

9. A later essay, published in the Surrealist journal *Minotaure,* states the case for "Le Merveilleux contre le mystère," Surrealism favoring the former. Breton seems to move gradually toward the side of the mystics; see the comments on *Arcane 17* and the essay "Du Surréalisme en ses oeuvres vives."

10. My source is Marie-Claire Dumas, the authority on Robert Desnos.

11. See the continuing proliferation of works on concrete poetry, combining the verbal and the visual, the witty and the serious.

Chapter Four

1. Pierre Reverdy, "L'Image," in *Nord-Sud* 13, March 1918.

2. See Marguerite Bonnet, *André Breton et la naissance de l'aventure surréaliste* (Paris: José Corti, 1983), p. 362 and *passim,* for a discussion of the Surrealist image.

3. *Signe ascendant,* December 30, 1947.

4. Here, as in all cases where the work has not yet entered the *Oeuvres complètes* of the Pléiade edition, I refer to the edition of Breton's works mentioned in the Bibliography.

Chapter Five

1. In the Pléiade edition, Marguerite Bonnet and the other editors comment on the background of the novel. The woman Nadja was real, born as Léona-Camille-Ghislaine D. near Lille in 1902; Breton met her after breaking with Lisa Meyer, the woman of the glove—a leather glove of palest blue, which he molds in bronze and keeps. It was in fact on his desk at 42 rue Fontaine.

Nadja wrote Breton a moving letter of separation, quoted in my text; in a letter
of 3 November 1926, she says to him: "You will use me, and I will do my best
to help you in something worthwhile" (*OC* I, 1511). Bored with Nadja's madness, Breton went on to love Suzanne Muzard, who eventually married
Emmanuel Berl but continued her affair with Breton. About the end of *Nadja,*
where she figures as X, she says: "I can't claim the end of *Nadja* as mine. This
text was set down in a burst of unreflective passion, as poetic as it was delirious,
and Breton should be honored for it, not me. Perhaps I had the talent for arous-
ing love, and Breton that of inspiring it, without having that magic talent of
being able to keep it up." Marcel Jean, *Autobiographie du surréalisme* (Seuil,
1978), 322; quoted in Breton's *OC* I, 1508.

2. There is a clear alternation in Surrealism between the will to share
the Surrealist experience and the contrary and sometimes simultaneous desire
not to distribute the *pain maudit aux oiseaux,* the damned and therefore sacred
bread of the movement to the sometimes ordinary birds who would devour it.
The contraries exist here, as in all dialectically based movements. Breton mentions here Lautréamont's personal disappearance behind his work, but for him
such a feat seems *supernatural* (always to be contrasted with the *surréel*); he himself, he implies, would not respect anyone who tried now to undertake the
same thing.

3. In another passage of *Nadja* (49), Breton explains his affection for
the Marché aux Puces as a place for finding, as one cannot in other places, certain objects which are "out of style, in pieces, useless, almost incomprehensible,
in short perverse in the sense I mean it and as I love the term." These objects,
like the "signal facts," can be put in no logical order and are a mockery of any
order we might wish to bestow on them.

4. Breton, in fact, accuses himself for having "betrayed" his own personal attraction to the actress Blanche Derval. Not to profit from all the "marvelous" sensations is to fall short of the Surrealist ideal.

5. There is no good translation for the French *"faire la part du feu"* (at
least, I have not found one here). It is a counsel of moderation: give something
its due, cut your losses, etc. Compare the following passage from *Les Vases communicants* (144): "To the extent that I got out of the way of cars, that I did not
permit myself to try out a firearm to see how it worked . . . I paid this world the
greatest compliment."

Chapter Six

1. Literally, a *fil conducteur,* a conducting wire; Breton is faithful to the
imagery of electricity. The same image is applied to the distant elements of an
image, and to any bringing together, an action to which Surrealism can be considered to have devoted itself in large part.

2. That the analysis should be carried on between two people fits,
of course, the traditional psychological pattern and is also highly appropri-

ate to Surrealism, which is more of a group phenomenon than an individual one.

3. Breton gives an interesting interpretation of the dream within a dream as (roughly speaking) a process of making more *unreal* that on which the dreamer would not want to confer the greater reality of the first-level dream.

4. Here Breton disavows his own greatness in any field at all.

Chapter Seven

1. *Point du jour, OC* II, 279. Hereafter cited in text as *PJ*.

2. Compare the equally definite style of "La beauté sera CONVULSIVE ou ne sera pas" (BEAUTY WILL BE CONVULSIVE OR NOT BE); see Hal Foster's *Compulsive Beauty* (Cambridge: M.I.T. Press, 1993).

3. Of course, this makes more sense applied to a country where dictations—*la dictée*—form a normal part of schoolwork.

4. Later, as Marguerite Bonnet will point out in her notes to this volume in the Pléiade, Breton will care more about the outside world, and so certain correspondences with the cosmos will matter more.

5. The *Femme 100 Têtes* also implies, by its sound, the *Femme Sans Tête*, or the *Headless Woman*.

Chapter Eight

1. From an article on Jacques Herold, in *Cahiers d'art* (October 1947); the comparison made at this point between the crystal and the coral (or the crystal in the sea) is doubly interesting in view of all of Breton's other references to the power of water—to the soluble fish, for instance, and to the water he imagines paralyzing the newest machines, imposing its own conditions from a position of greater strength.

2. There is often this total and obvious opposition, as discussed elsewhere. Compare this with other images, such as the one already mentioned of Noah's Ark, to which Breton would have the crow return instead of the dove, or that of the black sand he chooses as the ideal setting for his dreams, instead of the white sand he used to prefer.

3. As I did not upon writing the first version of this book.

4. Marguerite Bonnet, *André Breton et la naissance de l'aventure surréaliste* (Paris: José Corti, 1983), 22.

Chapter Nine

1. Marguerite Bonnet notes the continuity of this volume (*OC* II, 1559). It is clear even in the specific images, such as the "copper of Venus" in the second poem ("Quand tu marches le cuivre de Vénus/Innerve la feuille glis-

sante et sans bords"—"When you walk, the copper of Venus/Innervates the slippery rimless leaf"), for the alchemists used to call copper by the name of Venus because of its tendency to mix with other metals. Everything is in convergence, without rims and edges, in *The Air of Water*.

2. She is identified with—and not simply likened to—the flame: this is a vision of convergence, not of mere comparison. The first of these translations is by Mary Ann Caws; the second and third, by Mary Ann Caws and Jean-Pierre Caurin in their translation and edition of *Poems of Andre Breton* (Austin: University of Texas Press, 1982).

3. The visual balance is paralleled by the exact repetition of words.

4. A pun on earthworms: *"Vers de terre."*

5. Tristan Tzara, *Sept Manifestes Dada,* Pauvert, 1963, 107.

6. *"Bandeau"* refers to the blindfold in blindman's buff and at the same time to a diadem (allied to the notion of the marvelous). See also note 8.

7. Compare Eluard's *"ta langue dans le bocal de ta voix,"* "your tongue in the flagon of your voice."

8. Several of Breton's early poems have the rhythm and the vocabulary of Rimbaud; the voyage on the inside of the poet's eye is similar in feeling to the image of the young boy in Rimbaud's "Les Poètes de sept ans," who is *"écrasant son oeil darne,"* pushing on his eyelid to see interior visions. Compare with this poem the following:

> Sous le bandeau de fusées
>
> Il n'est que de fermer les yeux
>
> Pour retrouver la table du permanent (93)

> (Under the blindfold of rockets
>
> You only have to close your eyes
>
> To find again what stands lasting.)

9. Not "rediscover," since it is always for the first time.

10. For another circular poem, see "La Forêt dans la hache," "The Wood in the Hatchet."

11. Literally "open halfway," like the *"porte entr'ouverte"* in *Les Vases communicants:* it implies the marvelous and communication with it as the simpler *"ouvrir"* would not.

Chapter Ten

1. And Breton emphasizes the importance of the loss of an actual child (physical or psychological) in both Elisa's case and in his own.

Chapter Eleven

1.   For a discussion of the importance of electrical imagery in Breton's writings, see Julien Gracq, *André Breton, quelques aspects de l'écrivain,* José Corti, 1948. In his "Chasse spirituelle," Breton states categorically: "What matters to us is what determines the fusion of the mind and the heart into a verbal or plastic mold which shows itself from some perspective electrically appropriate to it" (*La Clé,* 140).

2.   Breton quotes here an article of Lo Duca, "L'Art et le fou."

3.   These listeners, or seers, are passive, in the sense that the medium is passive, in order to remain open to the message of the marvelous.

4.   In a footnote to this passage, Breton tells how the writer Raymond Roussel (a writer admired by the Surrealists) went much further in this way of thinking; having embarked for the South Seas, he then refused to get off the ship when it arrived at Tahiti, a marvelously funny-serious example of the unknown being preferred to the known.

5.   Bachelard is for this reason and others closely associated with Surrealism. For a more detailed account, see my *Surrealism and the Literary Imagination: Gaston Bachelard and André Breton* (The Hague: Mouton, 1966).

6.   See the discussion about the volume of Resistance poetry called *L'Honneur des poètes* and the essay repudiating it, *Le Déshonneur des poètes* by Benjamin Péret. The conception of honor is plainly different.

7.   From René Guénon, *Aperçus sur l'initiation,* quoted in Breton's essay "La Nuit du Rose Hôtel."

Chapter Twelve

1.   Part of a talk Breton gave at the Galeria de Arte de la Universidad de Mexico, for the opening of an exhibition of the works of Francisco Gutierrez (*OC* II, 1828).

Chapter Fourteen

1.   "Faire recevoir," an expression like Eluard's *"voir et faire voir," "donner à voir,"* etc. The image implies the seer sharing his vision, making seers of others, also.

2.   Breton's preface to Aimé Césaire, *Cahier d'un retour au pays natal,* (1947), 17.

Index

Titles in parentheses following the names of authors indicate those works most mentioned by the Surrealists.

The Author

Mary Ann Caws is a Distinguished Professor of English, French, and Comparative Literature at the Graduate School of City University of New York, and the Co-Director of the Henri Peyre Institute of the Humanities. She is the author of several books, essays, and journal articles on Surrealism and French literature and poetry, including *Surrealism and Literary Imagination* (1966), *The Poetry of Dada and Surrealism* (1971), and several volumes in Twayne's World Author Series including *André Breton* (1974), *René Char* (1976), and *Yves Bonnefoy* (1984).